SPEAKING OF GOD

SPEAKING OF GOD

Essays on Belief and Unbelief

edited by

DENIS DIRSCHERL, S.J.

105632

THE BRUCE PUBLISHING COMPANY/MILWAUKEE

Library of Congress Catalog Card Number: 67-24538

© 1967 THE BRUCE PUBLISHING COMPANY
MADE IN THE UNITED STATES OF AMERICA

Preface

The contemporary problem of belief, unbelief, and atheism, of man's relationship to God and the world, is a dominant preoccupation of the sixties. The problem, as old as prehistory itself, is a central theme — in all its myriad aspects — running through an unprecedented number of articles, books, movies, and plays. On the surface, it is as if man had reached that stage of awareness whereby he feels compelled to make an unalterable choice either for or against God. Today, as always, this option, as John Courtney Murray has pointed out, is unique in the sense that no man can claim that it is not his concern.

> If God is not, no one is permitted to say or even think that he is, for this would be a monstrous deception of oneself and of others. It would be to cherish and propagate a pernicious illusion whose result would necessarily be the destruction of man. On the other hand, if God is, again one thing is not permitted. It is not permitted that any man should be ignorant of him, for this ignorance, too, would be the destruction of man. On both counts, therefore, no man may say that the problem of God is not his problem.[1]

The crucial choice confronting all men, to affirm or to deny the existence and meaning of God, is the subject of this volume of essays. The work, it is hoped, will be a modest contribution to the current discussion of belief and unbelief. The main intent

---

[1] John C. Murray, S.J., *The Problem of God* (New Haven: Yale University Press, 1965), p. 4.

of the writers is to provide for an understanding and orientation to both the classical and modern treatment of the problems involved. This understanding, in turn, should not only insure a better appreciation or concern for the issues and real values being questioned in our own era, but it should also help urge us to face all men's common problems with the strength and courage that is now being demanded of us.

Father Mohler begins our work with his analysis of St. Augustine's explanation of faith, an explanation which certainly still remains one of the major contributions down through the centuries offered for solving the problems of belief and unbelief. Father Mohler centers chiefly on the great doctor's bipolar imperative: "Understand in order to believe, believe in order to understand." In its further development, while avoiding the extremes of both rationalism and fideism, we can penetrate Augustine's view of the dialectical collaboration of faith and reason. Unquestionably, Augustine's understanding of faith has much to tell all who are willing to ponder the message of his own profound experience of God's life in man.

The further enrichment of Augustine's interpretation of the faith-encounter by St. Thomas, where man's intellect and will engage in dialogue with God and his invitation to believe is the object of a second essay by Father Mohler. Here he highlights two of Thomas' notions of the faith-act: its interpersonal character and its dynamic initiation of eternal life. The value of these two essays consists in providing us not only with the historical background, the contextual framework within which the questions of faith and God were posed in the early and middle Christian tradition, but also with new insights for our times. Though there were numerous other formulations of faith and belief besides those of Thomas and Augustine, their contributions are the outstanding ones, and other men used these contributions as foundations for their own new ideas.

When we turn to men who opposed the Church's explanation of faith and belief, no one man's counter position has had such an impact on the world as that of Karl Marx. And though much ink has already been spilled on this subject, Marx's concept of belief and the non-existence of God bears further elaboration. For both East and West will have to treat this question much more seriously before there can be any real dialogue, any significant and lasting benefits from such a confrontation.

In the third essay of this volume I describe, by going back to the sources, Marx's attitude toward God and atheism. There are, of course, various opinions and interpretations given by specialists on this rock-bottom issue. The important point here is to discover what Marx thought and wrote about the subject of atheism. This is no small task indeed, and in some instances I have to be content with re-emphasizing key forgotten facts of Marx's world view. To be sure, there is really only a sniff of the original traces of Marx left in today's so-called communistic countries. Marx has been emasculated and for good reasons. Theory aside, the policies and practices of the Soviet Union and other Iron Curtain countries in the past decades also indicate the real importance given to atheism. In this respect the "Marxists" have been consistent.

Whether the early beginnings at dialogue now in process will blossom into a real meeting of minds remains to be seen. At any rate, both East and West will have to face squarely Marx's position that belief is a myth, non-rational, unreal — albeit difficult to dislodge from human consciousness. Marxists must also face up to the challenge of honestly considering the centrality of atheism, or more accurately, anti-theism in their philosophical system.

Moving from Marx's position, his eclectic synthesis of nineteenth-century European unbelief, Father Posadas illustrates the tremendous challenge which the Church faces in articulating and witnessing the faith in the contemporary world. As he writes, "In today's world there are no more Christian countries. To a large and increasing extent, there are no more Christian families where faith is handed down and accepted together with the family name, the family trade and the family fortune." Today the Church is faced with a serene, "self-confident atheism," an unbelief where "there are no disguises, no misunderstandings, no pretensions." Father Posadas continues by pointing out the real value atheism has for the contemporary Christian, its call for a Christian purification, and its emphasis and need of a freer, more authentic faith.

The "death of God" proponents and their radical theologies have already captured the attention of both the popular and technical mass media, most notably in 1965 and 1966. Professor Martin Marty and Father Stagaman tackle the problems this phenomenon presents, and they locate its development in the belief-unbelief context.

Father Stagaman explicates the main thrust of the ideas expounded by Thomas Altizer, John Robinson, and William Hamilton, three "philosopher-theologians" who so badly want to be men of their times. All three are searching and groping for the transcendent God who has disappeared, to their way of thinking, from the scene. Father Stagaman concentrates on Altizer's charge that Christ and his Kingdom has been obfuscated, radically disturbed in history, and that Christianity is not true to its origins.

Dr. Marty continues the analysis of the challenge of change in "God-talk" by Altizer, Hamilton and Van Buren. He uncovers the peculiar origins of the tensions and debate over transcendentalism and immanentism and offers an engaging inquiry into the development of the death of God movement to our day. He illustrates how easily historical processes can be set off into blind corners when a delicate, balanced, and reverent attitude toward science and Scripture is lacking. Both Dr. Marty's and Father Stagaman's essays reveal how vastly different are the questions posed about faith from century to century, even from decade to decade.

Professor Eugene Fontinell and Father Joseph Owens close this volume with a provocative discussion on the role of reason and metaphysics in belief. Underlying this discussion and a point that is uppermost in the whole question here is really the Church's adaptation to the changing world. In one sense Professor Fontinell is optimistic: "That the Roman Catholic Church is capable of change beyond the greatest expectations of friend and foe alike is now established beyond question." Just how

far will the Church go in her renewal and regeneration? What
are the criteria and limits to change, especially when considering the Church's relation to both the past and the future? These
are two questions that the reader will have to keep in mind
while reading the final two essays.

Professor Fontinell states that we should forget about old
criticisms against the Church and "take advantage of the freedom that now exists to bring forth positive ways of enriching
the life of the Church." In our current frame of mind, however,
he is frankly worried about our ability to integrate the "results
of the great revolutions in thought which have occurred over
the last four hundred years, and in particular those of the last
hundred years." On many important problems he believes that
our thought patterns and experience are opposed to the more
creative thinkers of our era. In this respect he exemplifies how
many non-Thomistic Catholic philosophers view the same subject today. For one thing he finds the "proofs" for the existence
of God unconvincing. In an age when personalism and "lived
experience" are emphasized, Fontinell asks for a halt to what
he terms the excess of rationalism in Catholic thought. Traditional metaphysics, in his view, has probably had its day, and
we are courting disaster by committing ourselves to one metaphysical framework.

Fontinell believes that an historical epoch like ours, in which
"the presence of God takes the form of a simultaneous and
terrifying absence of God," demands not only a change in
philosophical and theological terminologies or concepts but an
entirely new superstructure. And here, it seems, he has the
support of a growing number of Christians, the most recent and
notable being Leslie Dewart.[2] To avoid a stagnant, uncreative
thinking, Fontinell opts for a certain "wildness" of thought:
"What seems desperately needed is some free-wheeling hypothesizing on questions that are tearing out the insides of an increasing number of Catholics who fervently desire to be faithful
to the demands which contemporary thought and life make

---

[2] Cf. *The Future of Belief* (New York: Herder and Herder, 1966).

upon them and at the same time not to separate themselves from participation in the Church."

Father Owens raises the question whether to this day we have at all appreciated the real in-depth insight of St. Thomas. New critical studies, editions, and translations of the master schoolman's work, he notes, reveal a more meaningful voice for the problems of belief and unbelief in our contemporary world. He concludes that it would be dangerous, indeed, to throw overboard the basic concepts of Thomistic thought. In short, to win a new berth in the philosophical world it is not necessary to knock another star out of the sky. The constellation is large and another philosophy will not destroy the universe.

In Father Owen's view the basic truths of Thomas do admit of a structure for a creative philosophy, a philosophy that will not only not be supplanted, but, if better understood, will help solve problems confronting the Church and mankind for many years to come. To see God under the aspect of being, he believes, will be apropos and mandatory as long as man exists on this side of heaven, provided, that is, new insights are carefully incorporated within the given structure. Father Owens sees no reason to distrust human reason concerning not only the authenticity but also the importance of the demonstration of God's existence. In Father Murray's words, if the point is pushed to an extreme, "how odd of God it would have been had he made man reasonable so that, by being reasonable, man would become godless."[3]

The discussion about "God-talk" between Professor Fontinell and Father Owens closes this volume, but the debate and dialogue continues, for a faith which is truly alive necessarily remains critical of itself, probing, reaching out for new ways of expressing its life while moving along the road toward the culminating point, to the author of all. Until that goal is reached, man will be pressed to make the choice between the "dreadful news" of a Nietzsche or the "good news" of Christ, to face the challenge of straight thinking about God and honest living before God and man.   Denis Dirscherl, S.J.

---

[3] Murray, *op. cit.*, pp. 75–76.

Contents

SPEAKING OF GOD

~~~~~~

Thinking With Assent: The Theology of Faith of St. Augustine, An Interpretation

JAMES A. MOHLER, S.J., S.T.D.

The place of Augustine in the development of Western theology is undisputed. In fact, he has been called the first and last of the great Latin Doctors of antiquity.[1] An area of current interest is Augustine's contribution to Western theology of faith. In Augustine's theology we find a point of union between East and West, for it was Augustine who took Neoplatonism, sprung from Alexandria, and incorporated it into Western Christian thought. Both Origen, father of Eastern theology, and Plotinus, father of Neoplatonism, had studied in Alexandria under the great Ammonius Saccas in the third century. Perhaps in the affective, Neoplatonic strain of Augustine we may find a source of union with the affective theology of Eastern asceticism.

Augustine's Religious Experience

When we study Augustine's theology of faith, we see that it reflects his own religious experience, his search for the truth, and his conversion. Augustine, brilliant young student and educator, earnestly sought the truth through Manichaeism. Yet he was soon disillusioned by the ignorance of Faustus, whom he had admired from afar. Moreover, he soon tired of the skepticism of the Academics. It was in Neoplatonism that Augustine

---

[1] H. Marrou, *Saint Augustine* (New York: Harper, 1957), p. 154.

1

was to find a line of thought that appealed to him and which he felt was the truth. With Clement of Alexandria Augustine felt that there was some of God's truth in pagan authors.

The Neoplatonists inspired Augustine to begin his ascent to the Truth with the help of both a loving faith and reason.[2]

> After many centuries and much contention, a philosophy has finally been evolved which, in my opinion, is entirely true. It is not limited to this world — it reveals another, the intelligible world.[3]

The Neoplatonists also gave Augustine his solution to the problem of evil, releasing him from the materialism of Manichaeism, showing him that evil is really a privation of the good. Neoplatonism helped Augustine to see the wisdom of the gospel approach to spirituality. He was deeply impressed by the conversion of the Neoplatonist, Victorinus. Augustine's own conversion in 386 was a voluntary, loving assent which followed the intellectual preparation of Neoplatonism.[4]

Faith and Reason

The problem of faith and reason interested Augustine. He had sought the truth through reason, yet it was through reason enlightened by faith that he was to find it. Augustine never separated faith and reason, as more modern thinkers have done. He rather tried to penetrate by his understanding the Christian faith and to see the world and human life in the light of Christian wisdom.[5] Reason helps to bring a man to faith, and once a man has faith, reason aids him in penetrating the truths of faith. Based on his own experience, Augustine would say that reason helped him toward an understanding of what he believed, just as it had aided him on his way to faith.[6]

Augustine does not split man into the natural and supernatural, but treats him as he really is, that is, with a super-

---

[2] *Against the Academics*, 1. 3, c. 20, n. 43 (*PL* 32, 957). *PL* and *PG* refer to Migne's *Patrilogia Latina* and *Patrilogia Graeca* respectively.
[3] *Ibid.*, 1. 3, c. 19, n. 42 (*PL* 32, 956).
[4] F. Copleston, *A History of Philosophy*, Vol. 2, Part I (Garden City, N. Y.: Doubleday, Image, 1962), pp. 56–57.
[5] *Ibid.*, p. 63.
[6] *Concerning the True Religion*, c. 24, n. 45 (*PL* 34, 141).

natural end. Augustine is always interested in man in his concrete relationship with God here and now. Perhaps we can describe the Christian philosophy of Augustine as man's rational contemplation of Christian revelation: faith seeking understanding.

Faith and reason aid each other in pursuit of Christian wisdom. Reason plays an important part in faith, for it is only a reasoning, thinking creature, such as man, who can believe. "Understand in order to believe, believe in order to understand." This is the ever recurring motif of Augustine's theology. Augustine explains the cooperation of faith and reason in man's conversion in one of his sermons.

> From one aspect he is right when he says, "May I understand in order to believe." And I am right when I say with the Prophet, "Believe in order that you may understand." We both speak the truth and agree. Therefore, understand in order that you may believe; believe in order that you may understand. Briefly I explain how we can accept each other's opinion without controversy. Understand my word in order that you may believe. Believe God's word in order that you may understand.[7]

Understand my word that you should believe. This is the reasonable affirmation of the authority upon which faith is based. Certainly the authoritative words and example of Ambrose and Victorinus led Augustine to belief, but not without God's guidance. Faith is reasonable, for no one believes anything unless he first thinks it should be believed.[8]

Which comes first, faith or reason? As we have seen, Augustine did not clearly separate the two. Each aided the other on the road to beatitude.

> Therefore, it is reasonable that in great things which cannot be grasped, faith precedes reason. Of course, the reason, however small, which persuades this, antecedes faith.[9]

Reason somehow precedes faith, for only a rational man can

---

[7] *Sermon 43*, c. 7 (PL 38, 258).
[8] *Predestination of the Saints*, c. 2, n. 5 (PL 44, 963).
[9] *Epistle 120*, c. 1, n. 3 (PL 33, 453–454).

believe. Man's intellect must be capable of accepting the reasonable authority on which faith is based.

> For unless a man understands something, he cannot believe God. Nevertheless, by the very faith by which he believes, he is restored that he may understand more.[10]

Reason and faith work together, faith perfecting reason, leading it to further understanding. By our faith, our eyes are opened so that reason, purified by faith, can seek the truth. Faith builds on reason, elevates it so that man may attain the heights of understanding and vision. In faith God is unseen, yet the believer desires to see Him. Faith seeks understanding. Christ promised that those who believed in Him would see.

> What does he promise to believers, brothers? You will know the truth. What? Had they not known it when the Lord spoke? If they did not know, how did they believe? We believe in order to know, we do not know in order to believe. What we will know, "Eye hath not seen . . ." (Is 64, 4; 1 Cor 2, 9). What is faith, except to believe what you do not see. Truth is to see what you have believed.[11]

Faith is the necessary prelude to a partial understanding of revealed truths here below and the full vision of eternity.

Should we just accept revelation on faith alone without in any way seeking to understand what we believe? Augustine answers:

> Then you must revise your rule, not indeed to the extent of throwing your faith overboard, but to allow you to bring the light of reason to bear on what you already hold firmly by faith.[12]

"Faith seeking understanding" epitomizes Augustine's theology of faith. Faith, under the guidance of Christ, has a tension for understanding which will be complete only in the future vision.[13]

Is the faith of Augustine a prelude to understanding in the Manichaean sense, where the simple faith of the hearers was

10 *On Psalm 118*, c. 18, n. 3 (*PL* 37, 1552).
11 *In Jn.*, tr. 40, n. 9 (*PL* 35, 1690).
12 *Epistle 120*, c. 1, n. 2 (*PL* 33, 452).
13 *On Free Choice*, 1. 2, c. 2 (*PL* 32, 1243).

looked down upon as inferior to the superior gnosis of the elect? Augustine's faith is a necessary prerequisite to understanding, but it continues to work along with reason. Augustine's gnosis is a cooperative effort of God and man. God further enlightens the believer so that he can partially understand the revealed truths and eventually be united with Truth Himself in an everlasting vision.

Thinking With Assent

Augustine, reflecting the rapport between faith and reason, describes the act of faith as "thinking with assent."

> To believe is nothing more than to think with assent. Not every one who thinks, believes, since many think in order not to believe. But every one who believes, thinks. Believing, he thinks; and thinking, he believes.[14]

What is this "thinking" of Augustine? In his *Trinity* he describes "thinking" as a restless turning over of things of the mind.[15] Augustine's assent of faith resembled that of Clement of Alexandria.[16] This was not just an intellectual assent, but involved the whole man in a judgment of the truth and goodness of the object. So the affective power plays an important part in Augustine's faith.

In Augustine's act of belief, thinking precedes the assent. This mirrors Augustine's own experience, for he thought long and hard before he finally assented to Christ. However, thinking does not cease with the assent, but continues along with it, using reason perfected by faith in order to search for the understanding of the things believed. Both the intellectual and the affective powers of man cooperate in Augustine's faith-quest for the true and the good God.

Affective Faith

Augustine's whole theory of morality emphasized human affec-

---

[14] *Predestination of the Saints*, c. 2, n. 5 (*PL* 44, 963).

[15] *Trinity*, 1. 15, c. 16, n. 25 (*PL* 42, 1079), *In his Confessions* (1.10, c. 11 (*PL* 32, 787), he describes *"cogitatio"* as a "bringing together" (*Cogere*) of things hidden in the memory.

[16] *Stromata*, 7, 10 (*PG* 9, 481). See H. Wolfson, *The Philosophy of the Church Fathers* (Cambridge, Mass.: Harvard University Press, 1956), p. 129.

tivity, reflecting the gospels and the Neoplatonists.[17] Love played
an important part in his conversion. "Late have I loved Thee."[18]
From his own life, Augustine knew that man can either turn
away from God to the love of creatures, or he can turn toward
the good God in loving faith. Through faith man seeks the
beatifying vision of Truth, but he seeks it willingly and rejoices
in Him in charity.[19] In order for faith to be a virtue, it must
somehow act in the order of love.[20]

Following the Neoplatonists, Augustine taught the primacy of
the will in human knowledge. What is known cannot be divorced from what is loved. All cognition is somehow dependent
upon interest. Nothing is really fully known without the consent
of the will. Complete cognition lies with affection. The recognition of Christ through faith is primarily a movement of the will.
It is true that man's reason takes in and knows reality, both
eternal and temporal. But since reason is primarily passive and
neutral, it is directed by the will to recognize what it does
recognize. In Augustine the will is corrupt and needs cleansing
by faith in order to command the recognition of Christ.[21]

God must be primarily in the will, not the intellect, for the
intellect is under the will. In faith man conforms his will to
God's. Without faith man does not really know God well. He
does not recognize Him because he does not love Him. Men
use the divine light for science, but do not recognize the light.[22]
The Platonists were blind. They did not submit to God because
of perverted wills. Rather than submit to the inward illuminator,
they turned outwards to nature in search of God. It was love
and desire that they lacked, namely, the love and desire that
turn diffused awareness into true cognition.[23]

Augustine saw clearly the function of love in his own con-

17 F. Copleston, op. cit., 74, 94.
18 Confessions, 1. 10, c. 27, n. 38 (PL 32, 795).
19 In Jn., tr. 26, n. 44 (PL 35, 1607); tr. 29, n. 6 (PL 35, 1631).
Predestination of the Saints, c. 5 (PL 44, 968).
20 Customs of the Catholc Church, 1. 1, c. 5 (PL 32, 1322).
21 See R. Cushman, "Faith and Reason in the Thought of Augustine,"
Church History, 19 (1950), p. 274.
22 Ibid., p. 285.
23 Trinity, 1. 9, c. 12, n. 18 (PL 42, 970–971).

version. Intellectually he had ample knowledge of the gospels, yet he did not commit himself to God until his will was moved through the gift of faith. The noetic function of reason is dependent on the operation and direction of the practical and valuative reason, and the affections predispose theoretical reason and sensitive nature.[24] Here Augustine opposes Aristotle, for whom appetite follows intellect. [25] For Augustine, in knowledge as well as in faith, love precedes.[26] So man's awareness of God cannot pass to knowledge without desire.[27] However, since man's will is perverse, he turns from the divine light to creatures illuminated by the light. There follows an immoderate love of the senses, pride, and self-love.

Christ enlightens man, healing his sick will. He heals man's blindness, awakens him so that he can recognize God. He frees him from inordinate love of material things, from self-love. Christ moves the will through faith so that man can love the Good of which he was aware without acknowledging it. Humbled and purified by faith, man consents to the Truth and the Good.[28]

If one wants to understand correctly the sense of faith seeking understanding in Augustine, he should see how charity, or love, plays an important part in each aspect of inquiring faith. Man's reason seeking understanding, seeking greater purity and union with God, is voluntarily subordinated to Him and in charity rejoices in Him.[29]

Augustine taught a threefold belief, namely: to *believe* God (*credere Deo*), to believe *God* (*credere Deum*), and to believe *in* God (*credere in Deum*). The first is to believe that God speaks the truth, the second is to believe that He is God. The

---

[24] *In Jn.*, tr. 26, n. 4 (*PL* 35, 608).

[25] *The Soul*, 431a, 11; *Metaphysics*, 1072a, 30. See Cushman, *op. cit.*, p. 287.

[26] Cushman, *op. cit.*, p. 288.

[27] *Trinity*, 1. 9, c. 12, n. 18 (*PL* 42 970–971).

[28] *Trinity*, 1. 4, c. 18, n. 24 (*PL* 42, 904–905). See Cushman, *op. cit.*, p. 289.

[29] See R. Holte, *Béatitude et Sagesse, Saint Augustin et le problème de la fin de l'homme dans la philosophie ancienne* (Paris: Études Augustiniennes, 1962), p. 385.

third is to love Him,[30] and it is in this act that the living, loving faith of the believer is found. Commenting on John 6:29, "This is the work of God, that you believe in Him whom He has sent," Augustine writes that not every one who believes God believes in Him. For example, the demons believed Him, but did not believe in Him. "What is to believe in Him? Believing, to love; believing, to prize Him highly; believing, to go to Him and be incorporated in His members."[31] This is the faith acting through love described by the apostle (Gal 5:6). The difference between the faith of the unholy people and that of the elect is love.[32] In one of his sermons Augustine exhorts his hearers to charity rather than to faith, for if they have charity and love, they will have faith.[33] For Augustine to believe in Christ is an act of supernatural love, charity.

Light of Faith

Augustine taught an illumination theory of knowledge, rooted in Christian tradition and reflecting Plato and Plotinus. The divine light illumines the mind. It is the intelligible light in whom and by whom and through whom all those things which are luminous to the intellect become luminous.[34] For Plotinus the One, God, is the transcendent light, illuminating the minds of men. Augustine's theory of divine illumination is a theory of intuition and so of action. It is a theory of direct, immediate contact and participation in the divine light.[35]

Augustine demanded divine illumination because the human mind is changeable and temporal and needs help to see the unchangeable and eternal truths.[36] Only Changeless Truth Him-

---

[30] *Sermon on the Creed* (*PL* 40, 1190–1191). *On Psalm 77*, n. 8 (*PL* 36, 988). *On John*, tr. 29, n. 6 (*PL* 35, 1631).

[31] *In Jn.*, tr. 29, c. 7, n. 6 (*PL* 35, 1631).

[32] *Sermon 158*, c. 6 (*PL* 38, 865).

[33] *Sermon 90*, c. 8 (*PL* 38, 564).

[34] *Soliloquies*, 1. 1, c. 8, n. 15 (*PL* 32, 878). See also F. Copleston, *op. cit.*, p. 77.

[35] See C. Schuetzinger, *German Controversy on St. Augustine's Illumination Theory* (New York: Pageant, 1960), p. 79. See also É. Gilson, *Christian Philosophy of Saint Augustine* (New York: Random House, 1960), pp. 79, 92. Also see R. Holte, *op. cit.*, p. 313 ff.

[36] *On Psalm 119*, n. 4, 5 (*PL* 37, 1600). *Sermon 23*, c. 1 (*PL* 38, 155). See Copleston, *op. cit.*, p. 78.

self can illuminate us so that we can see. The divine light enables us to see the relationship of temporal things to the eternal truths. By it we can see the true meaning of creation, the world sustained, sanctified, and re-created by the Word Incarnate, in whose image it was made.[37]

Augustine compared the divine illumination of the soul to the light of the sun in the visible world. The sun, created facsimile of the divine light, shines on the visible world, enabling the eye to see. In a similar manner, God enlightens the mind, the eye of the soul, with an incorporeal light.[38]

Can man make use of this divine light outside of faith? Yes, he must in order to perceive the eternal truths. So the Platonists used the divine light. But they did not recognize it as divine light. Truly there is a vast gulf between being enlightened by God, and acknowledging the light. God is used by many, but only recognized by the few who go within themselves to discover the source of the light, the author and exemplar of the world, the Word Incarnate. It is only by faith that we can recognize the divine light and seek the beatifying union with the source of the light.

Purifying Light

Reflecting both the gospels and Plotinus,[39] Augustine taught the purifying effects of the divine light. The eye of the soul is sick and in need of healing, Augustine wrote in his *Soliloquies*.[40] The sick eye loves the darkness. It is the light of faith that purges the mind and cleanses it of earthly desires. As in Plotinus, so in Augustine purification is the reverse of illumination, culminating in union with the One, the Good, the source of the light. In Augustine illumination and purification seem to be simultaneous, for man is purified by the divine light. As the light is intensified, man is drawn into union with the source of the light. Union can be temporary as in mystical experiences or

---

[37] *City of God*, 1. 8, c. 6 (*PL* 41, 231). *Trinity*, 1. 12, c. 14, n. 22 (*PL* 42, 1009). See Cushman, *op. cit.*, pp. 277, 278.

[38] *Trinity*, 1. 12, c. 15 (*PL* 42, 1011).

[39] For example, John's prologue; Luke 11, 34–36; Plotinus, *Enneads*, 1. 1, c. 2, n. 4–6.

[40] 1. 1, c. 14, n. 25 (*PL* 32, 882).

eternal in the next life. The stress on purification, illumination, and affective union by Plato, Plotinus, and Augustine led the way for future developments in mystical theology.[41]

It is the healing light of faith that begins man's road to union and vision.

> Faith precedes reason, it cleanses the heart that it may bear the light of greater reason. Therefore, it is reasonably said by the Prophet, "Unless you believe, you will not understand" (Is 7, 9). In discerning these two, he meant that we believe so that we may be able to understand that which we believe.[42]

Belief is a necessary prelude to the partial understanding on earth and the full vision of eternity. With his mind purified by faith, man is free to go on to vision and union with divine Truth.

> Unless we walk by faith, we shall not be able to reach that vision which passes not, but abides, that vision which comes from our being fastened to truth by a purified mind.[43]

Eschatology of Faith

Faith begins our ascent to the Truth which culminates in beatifying union. Augustine, following the lead of Scripture, taught an eschatological faith. Quoting the Epistle to the Hebrews, he wrote of faith as the assurance of the things to be hoped for and the conviction of things not yet seen.[44] Augustine clearly taught the rapport between faith and vision. Faith is like the foundation of a house, or the root of a tree. The beautiful tree of beatitude grows from the humble root of faith.[45] The foundation of a house and the root of a tree are not pleasing to the eye. They are humble, yet they have a necessary rapport with their fulfillment. Thus humble faith is the foundation, the

---

[41] See J. Pieper, *Scholasticism*, tr. by R. and C. Winston (London: Faber and Faber, 1960), p. 51.
[42] *Epistle 120*, c. 1, n. 3 (*PL* 33, 453).
[43] *Christian Doctrine*, c. 2, n. 12 (*PL* 34, 43).
[44] *Enchiridion on Faith, Hope, and Charity*, c. 1, n. 18 (*PL* 40, 235).
[45] *In Jn.*, tr. 40, c. 8, n. 8 (*PL* 35, 1690).

beginning of eternal life. It is the root which will flower into beatitude.

Confessions: Story of Faith

Augustine's *Confessions* give us a good meditative account of his own conversion, of his own faith history. When he wrote, "Understand in order to believe; believe in order to understand," he may well have been thinking of himself and how he had studied Plotinus and read the gospels and listened to Ambrose, Alpius, and Nebridius. "Understand in order to believe." After his conversion, he sought understanding through faith. "Believe in order to understand."

Augustine himself experienced the way of purgation, illumination, and union. With God's help he was cleansed from sin and from earthly desires. The divine light grew stronger as he was purged of philosophical and theological error. By the grace of God, he experienced a conversion to a union with the true and the good God.[46] The natural light grew stronger with conversion, as supernatural light is added to the natural light of reason. The stronger the light, the more purified he becomes and the closer his union with the source of the light.[47]

Certainly the I-Thou theme of the *Confessions* illustrates Augustine's striving for union. "You have made us for yourself, and our heart is restless until it rests in you."[48] For Augustine faith represented the perfect security of mind and heart he had struggled for through so many years. And now he felt the need to communicate his triumph of certitude and to share it with all who seek the same beatitude.[49]

Summary of Augustine's Theology of Faith

Augustine's whole life had been a search for the Truth, first as a student of Manichaeism, then as an Academic, and as a Neoplatonist. But it was only through faith that he was to find

---

[46] See J. Ryan, tr., *Confessions of Saint Augustine* (Garden City: Image, 1960), p. 29.

[47] *Ibid.*, p. 30.

[48] *Confessions*, 1. 1, c. 1, n. 1 (*PL* 32, 661).

[49] See A. Brunhumer, "The Heart of Augustine's Confessions," *Thought* 37 (Spring, 1962), 126.

the divine Truth, the exemplar and cause of all true things. It is Christ Himself who is in a very special way God's begotten Truth.

Augustine was convinced of the rapport between faith and reason. Faith and reason complement each other. "Understand in order to believe, believe in order to understand." Faith leads the way toward an understanding of the things that we believe. Yet somehow reason precedes faith, for one must understand something in order to believe. In faith, reason continues to strive for the vision of the unseen Truth, in spite of the firm assent. So faith can properly be described as "thinking with assent."

The assent of faith is a willing one. Augustine taught the importance of the affective power in faith. Interest precedes knowledge. Unless a man's sick will is healed, he cannot turn from love of creatures to the love of God. It is the affective belief in God which separates the believers from the unholy people. Belief in God is a loving belief, inspired by charity.

Augustine's faith is an illuminating faith, reflecting the gospels and Neoplatonism. It is Christ, the Truth Incarnate, who illumines the soul through faith. It is the light of faith that purifies the heart that it may bear the light of greater reason, leading man toward union with the divine light. By the light of faith man can not only see the eternal truths, but also recognize the divine light. It is by faith that man can recognize in the world the reflection of the divine ideas according to which it was made. It is through faith that man recognizes the image and end of creation. Far from separating man from the secular world, faith helps him to appreciate its true image and end, divine Truth.

Augustine's Theology of Faith in the Middle Ages

Medieval tracts on faith reflected Augustine strongly, even after the trend toward Aristotle in the middle of the thirteenth century.[50] God as First Truth, revealing and revealed, and His Divine Son as Begotten Truth were frequent themes in medieval

---

[50] H. Marrou, *op. cit.*, p. 158.

theology. Augustine's rapport between faith and reason can be found in many medieval authors, for example, Anselm's "Faith seeking understanding." Faith and reason aid each other in the pursuit of the Truth.

Augustine's classical description of belief, "Thinking with assent," is found in most medieval treatises on faith. Augustine's Neoplatonic illumination theory of knowledge was popular especially before Thomas Aquinas. This developed into the light of faith as taught by men like William of Auxerre and Thomas Aquinas. Augustine's threefold belief was discussed by most medieval theologians. Like Augustine, they seemed to emphasize loving belief in God as the keystone to faith. Earlier theologians tended to place more stress on the affective side of faith in contrast to the later more intellectual faith of Aquinas.

The ascetical tradition of medieval times and that of the later Spanish mystics reflects the way of purification, illumination, and union of Augustine. This agrees with Augustine's basic eschatology of faith. Faith has a rapport with vision, it is the beginning of eternal life.

Even though Thomas Aquinas' theology of faith tends to emphasize the intellectual side as determined by the divine object, First Truth, nevertheless, all of the Augustinian teachings mentioned above can be found in Thomas' tract on faith. Thomas' theology of faith is, as Grabmann said, an Aristotelian transport of Augustinian faith.[51]

Perhaps a thorough study of Augustine's faith will be a help to the ecumenical movement today, for the faith of the Reformers and that of the Eastern churches both show an affective nature reminiscent of Augustine. As Augustine played such a large part in the discussions of Trent,[52] so, too, he must be at the foundations of serious discussions on reunion.

---

[51] "Augustins Lehre von Glauben und Wissen und ihr Einfluss auf das mittelälterliche Denken," in *Aurelius Augustinus* (Cologne: Bachem, 1930), pp. 87–110.

[52] H. Marrou, *op. cit.*, p. 165.

The Dynamic Faith of Thomas Aquinas

JAMES A. MOHLER, S.J., S.T.D.

Today the theology of faith emphasizes the personal, seeking refuge from the abstract, dialectical faith of the scholastics. Faith today is a personal, existential, phenomenological relationship, the I-Thou rapprochement between man and God, right now, in man's own particular existential circumstances.[1] Is the faith of Thomas Aquinas foreign to the I-Thou of Buber, the ultimate concern of Tillich, or the personal faith of Cirne-Lima? As we shall see, the overly intellectual, dialectical, dessicated faith often attributed to Catholic tradition is not that of Thomas.

When we examine the teachings of Thomas Aquinas, we find that, far from being abstract and sterile, they describe a living, existing faith in which man has a personal relationship with God, the First Truth, here and now. Faith is the beginning of eternal life. The dynamism which begins in faith now will be perfected and completed in vision then.

Can Thomas' faith be called existential in any way at all? Certainly he wrote of a living, existing faith in which the hoped for things pre-exist in man here and now. However, to equate existence in Thomas' faith with the *Dasein* of the existentialist

---

[1] See M. Buber, *I and Thou* (New York: Scribners, 1958); P. Tillich, *Dynamics of Faith* (New York: Harper, 1958); G. Marcel, *Being and Having* (New York: Harper, 1965); C. Cirne-Lima, *Personal Faith* (New York: Herder and Herder, 1964).

14

might cause problems. Although Thomas speaks of an existing faith, he does not teach specifically of the faith of this or that concrete individual here and now. The faith of Thomas is an existing, living faith, yet it does abstract from individual existential circumstances, thus attaining a universal faith, applicable to all men in various time and circumstances. Existential faith, on the other hand, seems to stress the uniqueness of each man's faith-relationship with God.

Modern existential faith differs from that of Thomas Aquinas in still another way: in concentrating on the existential, personal, and subjective, it sometimes neglects the eschatological, the tension for vision, which is so essential to Thomas' faith. Faith for Thomas not only is a living, existing, personal relationship with First Truth but it also has an essential rapport with vision. It is the real beginning of eternal life, the pre-existence and anticipation of beatitude, for which man continually strives under the guidance of a loving charity.

The Classical Formula of Faith

It is perhaps in his study of the classical formula of faith in the Epistle to the Hebrews[2] that we can find the secret of Thomas' faith, for here is found faith's true, existential dynamism for vision, its fundamental rapport with beatitude. The classical formula states that faith is the substance (*substantia*) or assurance of the things to be hoped for. It is the evidence (*argumentum*) or conviction of the things unseen. Thomas follows tradition in calling faith the substance or the foundation of the whole spiritual life, just as light is the substance or basis of color.[3] In his *De Veritate* he explains faith as the

---

[2] *In Hebr.*, 11, 1. Abbreviations of Thomas' works quoted here are as follows:

    3S — *Commentary on the Third Book of the Sentences.*
    D.V. — *De Veritate.*
    S.C.G. — *Summa Contra Gentiles.*
    C.T. — *Compendium Theologiae.*
    In Hebr, In Jn, etc. — *Commentaries on Scripture.*
    De Vir. — *De Virtutibus.*
    Quodl. — *Quaestiones Quodlibetales.*
    In Boeth. de Trin. — *Commentary on Boethius' "De Trinitate."*
    S.T. — *Summa Theologiae.*

[3] *3S*, d. 23, a. 1, ad 1.

substance of things to be hoped for insofar as it is the first beginning of these things. Just as the foundation of a house or the hull of a ship is the substance or the first beginning of the completed structure, so faith is the real beginning of and initial participation in eternal life.[4]

Since eternal life consists in a full knowledge of God, there must pre-exist in faith some initial participation in this knowledge. It is this pre-existence which is the beginning of eternal life.[5] The inchoative knowledge mirrored in the human mind by the light of faith contains, in an incipient way, the things to be hoped for as the conclusions of science are contained virtually in their principles.[6]

Thomas often compared man's rapport with God in faith to that of a student with his teacher.

> Hence, in order that a man arrive at perfect vision of heavenly happiness, he must first of all believe God, as a disciple believes the master who is teaching him.[7]

In the liberal sciences, the principles must first be learned from the teacher. In these principles the whole science is contained in a germinal manner, just as conclusions are contained in their premises and effects in their causes. Thus he who learns the principles of science from his teacher has the substance of it. Similarly one who believes God has the substance of the full knowledge of vision which is contained virtually in his faith.

So in Thomas' explanation of faith as the substance of the things to be hoped for, we see faith's existential eschatology expressed as the anticipated possession, the pre-existing proportion, the incipient knowledge of the things to be hoped for. In faith, the hoped-for things somehow subsist in us now.[8]

---

[4] *D.V.*, q. 14, a. 2.
[5] *Ibid.*
[6] *In Hebr.*, 11, 1.
[7] *S.T.*, 2–2, q. 2, a. 3. *Also 3S*, d. 23, q. 2, a. 1, s. 4; *D.V.*, q. 14, a. 10, 11; *S.C.G.*, c. 152; *In Hebr.*, 11, 1; *S.T.*, 2–2, q. 4, a. 1; *In Jn.*, c. 5, l. 4, n. 5.
[8] For further discussion of the eschatology of faith in Hebrews, see C. Spiq, *L' épître aux Hébreux* (Paris: Gabalda, 1953), p. 336 ff.; E. Grasser, *Der Glaube im Hebräerbrief* (Marburg [Marburger Theologische Studien, 2]: Elwert, 1965), pp. 171–184.

In the second part of the classical formula, faith is seen as the evidence or conviction of the things unseen. It is a proof from the infallible authority of God. It is a foretaste of the full knowledge of vision as the foreword of a book is a prelude to what follows. This second part of the Hebrews' formula complements the first so that both together show the rapport of the will and the intellect with their divine object in the act of faith. Faith is both the substance and the conviction of the future vision of the unseen, but hoped-for, divine object.[9]

Thomas' Formula of Faith

Thomas took the description of faith in Hebrews and expressed it in his own words, calling faith, "The habit of the mind whereby eternal life is begun in us, making the intellect assent to those things which are not apparent."[10] Eternal life begins in us *now* with the habit of faith. Here is expressed concisely the existential and eschatological dynamism of Thomas' faith. Eternal life begins in us now and will be perfected and completed in the vision of beatitude.

Thomas frequently describes faith as a *"praelibatio"* or a foretaste of vision.[11] This seems to indicate the savorous knowledge of the virtue of faith, the firm foundation of the spiritual edifice.[12] The knowledge of God, then, that we have through our faith is a foretaste, a prelude, an anticipation, a guarantee, a beginning, a pre-existing proportion of that in which we will fully participate in vision.

First Truth

If faith is the beginning of eternal life, then the direct object of faith should be that whereby man is made one of the blessed. The divine object takes the prime place in Thomas' theology of faith, for it is First Truth who specifies the supernaturality of the act and habit of faith. Moreover, it is First Truth who

---

[9] *D.V.*, q. 14, a. 2; *In Hebr.*, 11, 1; *S.T.*, 2–2, q. 4, a. 1.
[10] *D.V.*, q. 14, a. 2; *In Hebr.*, 11, 1; *S.T.*, 2–2, q. 4, a. 1.
[11] 3S, d. 23, q. 2, a. 1, ad 4; *D.V.*, q. 14, a. 2, ad 9; *C.T.*, c. 1; *S.C.G.* 4, c. 54; *In Jn.*, c. 15, 1. 3, n. 3.
[12] *In Jn.*, c. 3, 1. 3; *In 1 Cor.*, c. 3, 1.2.

determines that faith reside in the speculative intellect.[13] It is
fitting that both faith and beautitude consist primarily in specula-
tion, for the one is the beginning of the other. Thomas' theology
of beatitude in contemplation is based on Aristotle.[14] The placing
of faith in the speculative intellect ties faith in with beatitude
and also gives Thomas' theology of faith an intellectual slant,
although he gives an important place to the will, insisting that
faith resides in the speculative intellect only insofar as it is
moved by the will.[15]

Thomas teaches an object-centered faith. Following Aristotle,
he describes the importance of the object in specifying acts
and habits.[16] Thus the divine object, First Truth, determines
or specifies the supernatural nature of the act and habit of
faith. He is not merely a passive object, but actively invites
man to believe and enlightens his faith.

First Truth is the object and medium of our faith. The Old
Testament tells us that Israel believed and relied upon Yahweh
because He was true to His promise. He is the true God.
Following this tradition, passed on by the Fathers and theologians, Thomas calls First Truth — the true God, the exemplar
and cause of all things that are true — the medium of our faith.
He is the whole reason of our faith. He reveals Himself to us
and we know that He cannot lie. Upon this our faith is based.
Credimus Deo. We believe God, First Truth, revealing.[17]

Nothing comes under a power, habit, or act, except through
the medium of the formal reason of the object (*mediante ratione
formali objecti*).[18] In faith, First Truth is the formal reason of
the object. It is because of Him that we believe.

Accordingly, if in faith we consider the formal reason of

---

[13] *S.T.*, 2–2, q. 4, a. 2, ad 3.
[14] *S.T.*, 1–2, q. 3, a. 5. Aristotle, *Nic. Eth.*, 1. 10, c. 7, n. 9 (1178 a, b).
See D. Emmet, "Theoria and the Way of Life," *Journal of Theological
Studies*, 17 (April, 1966), pp. 38–52.
[15] *S.T.*, 1–2, q. 56, a. 3; *De Vir.*, q. 1, a. 7; *D.V.*, q. 14, a. 4, *S.T.*
1–2, q. 57, a. 1.
[16] *S.T.*, 1–2, q. 18, a. 2; q. 54, a. 1, 2, 3. Aristotle, *Politica*, 3, 4, 2,
1276b, 31); *Nic. Eth.*, 7, 8, 4 (1151a, 16); *Meta.*, 5, 20 (1022b).
[17] *S.T.*, 2–2, q. 2, a. 2; *also* 3S, d. 23, q. 2, a. 2, q. 2; *D.V.*, q. 14, a. 7.
[18] *S.T.*, 2–2, q. 1, a. 3; q. 8, a. 3, ad. 2.

the object, it is nothing else than First Truth, for the faith of which we are speaking does not assent to anything except because it is revealed by God.[19]

First Truth is the very medium of our faith.

Although we are led to creatures by reason of First Truth, through it we are led mainly to First Truth itself, since it gives witness primarily about itself. So in faith First Truth acts as medium and object.[20]

Because of the infallibility of First Truth we give our assent of faith.[21] Thus our assent is firm and certain.[22]

God as First Truth invites us to believe. And, having given us the invitation, He enlightens our way to belief. The interior help of God as First Truth is the key to the dynamism of Thomas' faith, for here First Truth specifies the act and habit of faith, the habit of faith perfecting the intellect and acting as the supernatural principle of the acts.

Thomas called First Truth's interior help in the art of faith the interior instinct, the divine calling, invitation, and motion. It is Christ, First Truth, who invites, teaches, and illumines man through the interior instinct.[23] The interior instinct of faith is more important than external helps such as miracles and preaching.[24] The interior instinct to believe seems to be something more than the habit of faith, namely, whatever divine aid inclines man to believe.[25] The interior instinct is an interior speaking, inviting, whereby the unseen First Truth calls man to Himself.[26]

Following the gospels, the Fathers, and the theologians, Thomas also called First Truth's interior help the light of faith. Is the light of faith the same as the interior instinct to believe?

---

[19] *In Boeth. de Trin.*, q. 3, a. 1, ad 4.
[20] *D.V.*, q. 14, a. 8, ad 9.
[21] *S.T.*, 2–2, q. 2, a. 2; q. 4, a. 5, ad 2.
[22] *D.V.*, q. 10, a. 12, ad 6.
[23] 3S, d. 23, q. 2, a. 2, s. 3; *Quodl.*, 2, q. 2, a. 1, ad 3; *In Jn.*, c. 6, 1. 5, n. 3.
[24] *S.T.*, 2–2, q. 10, a. 1, ad 1.
[25] *In Jn.*, c. 6, 1. 4, n. 7.
[26] See J. Alfaro, "Supernaturalitas Fidei Iuxta S. Thomam, II: Functio 'Interioris Instinctus,'" *Gregorianum* 44 (1963), 765–766.

Thomas seemed to indicate a close link between the two.[27] In faith First Truth not only invites man to believe, but also illumines his mind so that he can give a firm assent to First Truth, even though He is unseen. He enlightens man's intellect, stamps it with His seal, specifying the act of faith as of and toward First Truth.[28]

The light of faith is really the habit of faith itself,[29] illuminating the articles.[30] Yet even with this interior help, man still does not see perfectly, not because of any defect in the divine light, but rather because of his imperfect participation in the light.[31] The light of faith does not destroy the natural light, but rather strengthens it.[32] It elevates man so that he can see in a concrete manner that it is good here and now to believe God.[33] Moreover, the light of faith helps man to see the dynamic eschatology of faith, so that he can tend toward the vision of First Truth, and, understanding this tendency, he may adhere simply First Truth through an assent proportioned to the dignity of God revealing. The light of faith for Thomas is the very habit of faith, conferring on the assent of faith the highest firmness of adhesion, superior to that of natural certitude.[34]

Man of himself is insufficient to assent to the unseen and transcendent First Truth. He needs the help of First Truth to aid his assent by inviting and illuminating him interiorly so that he can adhere imperfectly in the unseen First Truth through faith in order to adhere in Him perfectly in vision.

As in Thomas' discussion of the classical formula of faith, so also in his explication of the divine object, First Truth, the existential and eschatological dynamism of faith is evident.

---

27 *Quodl.*, 2, q. 4, a. 1, ad 3; In *Boeth. de Trin.*, 1, q. 1, a. 1, ad 4. Fr. Alfaro (*op. cit.*) calls the interior instinct an actual motion of faith which proceeds from the habit. It is the infused habitual inclination in second act. 763.

28 *Quodl.*, 2, a. 6, ad 3; In *Boeth. de Trin.*, 1, q. 1, a. 1, ad 4.

29 3S, d. 23, q. 2, a. 1; In *Boeth. de Trin.*, 1, q. 1, a. 1, ad 4.

30 In 1 *Sentence*, prol.; q. 1, a. 3, q. 3, s. 2.

31 *D.V.*, q. 14, a. 1, ad 5.

32 *S.T.*, 1, q. 12, a. 13.

33 *S.T.*, 2–2, q. 1, a. 5, ad 1.

34 See J. Alfaro, "Supernaturalitas Fidei luxta S. Thomam, I: Functio 'Luminis Fidei'," *Gregorianum* 44 (1963), p. 542.

It is the same First Truth who is both the unseen object of faith here and now and who will be the seen object of beatitude. He it is who reveals Himself to man externally and internally invites and enlightens man toward eternal life through faith.

Thinking With Assent

The inward invitation of the unseen First Truth provides the act of faith with its eschatological drive, for the very heart of the act is a ceaseless striving to see the divine object. Augustine described the act of faith as thinking with assent, in which man, despite his firm assent, still thinks, seeking to understand the hidden mysteries of faith.[35] Thinking with assent is both existential and eschatological. What could be more existential than the act of thinking? What could be more eschatological than the dynamic striving for vision of the discursive thought of faith?

The thinking of the act of faith is not scientific thought which is the cause of the assent and ceases once the assent has been given. No, it is a discursive thought which perdures along with the firm assent. Faith is, in a sense, a medium between two thoughts. One inclines the will to believe, and this precedes faith. The other tends to the understanding of those things which it believes, and this is along with the assent of faith.[36]

The intellect does not rest satisfied in faith; it still thinks discursively and inquires about the things it believes although its assent to them is unwavering. Since the understanding is dissatisfied and terminated from without, a movement directly opposite to what the believer holds firmly can arise.[37] The thinking of faith is the movement of the mind while yet deliberating and not yet perfected by the clear vision of truth.[38]

The discursive thought of faith will remain restless and dissatisfied until men can see First Truth in beatitude. This rest-

---

[35] *Predestination of Saints,* c. 2, n. 5 (*PL* 44, 962).
[36] *3S,* d. 23, q. 2, a. 2, s. 1, ad 2.
[37] *D.V.,* q. 14, a. 1.
[38] *S.T.,* 2–2, q. 2, a. 1.

lessness and this dissatisfaction are an integral part of faith and distinguish it from science and understanding where the intellect rests satisfied; whereas the firm assent of faith clearly separates it from doubt and opinion.[39] Since the object is unseen, the intellect remains dissatisfied, for the intellect is made to see.[40] Thus our intellectual operation in faith remains imperfect.[41] Moreover, this imperfect knowledge is essential to faith.[42]

But why does not God give man perfect knowledge of Himself here below? Is this not a defect on God's part? The imperfect knowledge of faith is not, for Thomas, due to any defect on the part of God; rather the defect lies in man whose weakened intellect cannot participate perfectly in God's knowledge here below. But man is dissatisfied with the imperfect knowledge of faith and restlessly strives to see the unseen object. Here is the kinetic eschatology of Thomas' faith, namely, the discursive thought ceaselessly yearning for vision. Through his faith, the beginning of eternal life, man seeks the full knowledge of beatitude, the perfection of eternal life.

While the intellect is assenting to the unseen First Truth, at the same time, urged on by the will, it strives restlessly for vision. So the act of faith is more than an intellectual assent. It is an affective knowledge, for in belief the will sustains, vivifies, and informs faith by love.

Charity Perfects the Dynamism of Faith

After having discussed the object and act of faith in his *Summa*,[43] Thomas goes on to explain the habit of faith, the principle of the acts.[44] It is in the virtuous habit of faith, formed by charity, that we find the perfection of faith's eschatological dynamism, for charity gives to the virtue of faith its perfect direction to beatitude.

---

[39] 3S, d. 23, q. 2, a. 2, s. 1; *D.V.*, q. 14, a. 1; *S.T.*, 2–2, q. 2, a. 1.
[40] *D.V.*, q. 14, a. 1, ad 5; *S.T.*, 2–2, a. 2, a. 3.
[41] *S.C.G.*, 3, c. 40.
[42] *S.T.*, 1–2, q. 67, a. 3.
[43] *S.T.*, 2–2, q. 1–3.
[44] *Ibid.*, q. 4.

In the act of faith, First Truth draws man to Himself, man's intellect assenting at the command of the will. Yet the will must be rectified, perfected by charity in order to command the assent of faith and to direct it in a perfect manner toward the final vision. Charity directs faith to beatitude and will continue in beatitude where faith will no longer exist. Charity rectifies the will in faith and in beatitude and thus serves as an effective and affective link between faith and vision.[45]

Charity informs the dynamism of faith, the loving will urging the intellect toward God (*in Deum*) in a perfect manner. Augustine describes this belief in God (*credere in Deum*) as a loving faith, accompanied by charity.[46] Thomas seems to teach a twofold "*credere in Deum.*" Besides that of charity, there is another *élan* which does not proceed from this virtue and which alone is essential to faith. This motion of the will is necessary even for an act of formless faith, for if the intellect is to assent, it must be moved by the will.

This initial affection for God in faith Thomas calls "a certain appetite for the promised good."[47] This incipient and imperfect appetite is distinguished from charity, which is a perfect and disinterested tendency. "*Credere in Deum*" for Thomas is not only that which is essential to faith and pertains to the will; it is also the virtue of charity perfecting the dynamism of faith in its proper movement toward its divine end.[48]

The initial movement of the will in faith, "*credere in Deum,*" is perfected by charity, the form of the virtues. In his theology of the virtue of faith, Thomas follows his teachings on the virtues in general, namely, that charity informs the acts of all the supernatural virtues, orienting them in a perfect manner to their last end. Without charity, these acts do not have their

---

[45] *Ibid.*, 1–2, q. 4, a. 4.
[46] *In Jn.*, tr. 29, c. 7, n. 6 (*PL* 35, 1631).
[47] *D.V.*, q. 14, a. 2, ad 10; *S.T.*, 2–2, q. 4, a. 7; q. 5, a. 2, ad 2.
[48] At times Thomas seems to identify "*credere in Deum*" with formed faith: *D.V.*, q. 28, a. 4, ad 6; *In Jn.*, c. 1, 1. 15; c. 6, 1. 13; *In Rom.*, c. 4, 1. 2. However in the *Summa*, he writes that "*credere in Deum*" signifies the intellect as moved by the will in the act of faith: *S.T.*, 2–2, q. 2, a. 2. See J.-M. Parent, "La signification du 'credere in Deum' chez saint Thomas," *Études et Recherches*, 9 (1955), 149–155.

Godward direction except in an incipient and imperfect manner. This ordination to the end is the form of the acts, for form directs to end. The will initiates all moral acts and the object and quasi-form of the will is the will's end. Whatever gives an act its order to an end in moral acts, also gives it its form. Since charity gives form and direction to the acts of the other virtues, it gives form to them by applying them to its end.[49]

Charity acts in a similar manner toward the virtue of faith, informing the acts of faith and ordering them to its end, which is God.[50] Thomas calls charity a kind of exemplary form[51] or an effective form of faith.[52] Charity gives the acts of faith their perfect God-direction toward beatitude,[53] granting man a foretaste of the future vision.[54] It is this dynamic faith, formed by charity, that is the foundation of the whole spiritual edifice culminating in glory.[55]

Personal Faith

Thomas' faith is dynamic in its definition, object, act, and formation. It is both an existential and an eschatological faith insofar as it is the real beginning of eternal life here and now. However, is not the faith of Thomas abstract and desiccated? Even the terminology smacks of the dialectic: substance, things to be hoped for, First Truth, formal object, act, habit, form. Medieval theologians have been accused of depersonalizing faith in their attempts to analyze it. Roger Aubert writes that the scholastics tended to emphasize the global aspect of faith so that faith became not so much a rapport between an individual believer and God, but rather a collective relationship between the Church and God.[56]

[49] S.T., 2–2, q. 23, a. 8; De Caritate, a. 3.
[50] 3S, d. 23, q. 3, a. 1, q. 1; D.V., q. 14, a. 5; S.T., 2–2, q. 4, a. 3.
[51] D.V., q. 14, a. 5.
[52] S.T., 2–2, q. 23, a. 8, ad 1.
[53] S.T., 1–2, q. 67, a. 6.
[54] 3S, d. 23, q. 1, a. 1, ad 4; D.V., q. 14, a. 2, ad 9; C.T., 1; S.C.G. 4, c. 54; In Jn., c. 15, 1. 3, n. 3.
[55] S.T., 2–2, q. 4, a. 7, ad 4; also 1–2, q. 89, a. 2, ad 2; In Jn., c. 3, 1. 3.
[56] R. Aubert, "Le caractere raisonnable de l'acte de foi chez les theologiens de la fin du XIIIe siecle," Revue d'Histoire Ecclésiastique, 39 (1943), 22–99.

Thomas Aquinas, too, has been accused of depersonalizing faith. It is true that Thomas took an objective view of faith; it is true also that he abstracted from experiential circumstances in order to obtain a universal faith. Nevertheless, since he based his teachings on Scriptures and the Fathers, perhaps it would be within his mind to interpret some of his faith doctrine in a personalistic manner,[57] being careful not to interpret his writings according to problems that are more in common with our own times than with his.

Some would feel that the act of faith today is more of a personal decision for Christ than it was in medieval times. However, although Thomas analyzed faith in an abstract way, nevertheless in the background is always the personal union between God and man. Thomas' faith is fundamentally a living, believing, experiential faith.

The personal God reveals Himself to man and is believed. "Hence faith which through assent unites man to divine knowledge has God as its principle object and everything else as a subsequent addition."[58] Thus the principle role in belief is the person to whom assent is given. Secondary are the truths that he proposes for our belief.[59] The revealed truths of faith come to us from God, who alone can see the divine secrets and teach them to us.[60] The personal God reveals Himself to man because He loves him. But why is the revelation obscure? Not because of a lack of love on God's part. Rather it is because of the weakness of man's intellect.

The object of faith, then, is a personal being, who is both truth and beatitude.[61] Faith foreshadows the personal beatific union of glory. Thomas' First Truth is not an abstract truth,

---

[57] R. Aubert, *Le Problème de l'acte de foi* (Paris: Warny, 1958), p. 622. Fr. Copleston in his *Contemporary Philosophy* (London, Burns and Oates, 1963), 104, reminds us that "person" did not mean the same for medieval scholastics as it does for modern thinkers. For a personalistic interpretation of Thomas' faith see J. Mouroux, *I Believe* (New York: Sheed & Ward, 1959).

[58] *D.V.*, q. 14, a. 8.

[59] *S.T.*, 2-2, q. 11, a. 1.

[60] *S.C.G.*, 3, c. 154; *S.T.*, 2-2, q. 6, a. 1.

[61] *S.T.*, 2-2, q. 5, a. 1.

but a subsistent Truth, personal God, under the title or aspect of First Truth. He is both the cause and the object of belief. He it is who invites man to believe and illumines him so that he can firmly assent and adhere in the unseen First Truth as the formal object of his faith.[62]

Thomas' faith is interpersonal. The divine Person reveals Himself and the human person believes. In the background of Thomas' tract on faith it is man, the person, who is the principle of his acts, directing them freely toward his last end.[63] The whole man believes, not just his intellect and will. In the intercommunion of faith, love and knowledge are, in a sense, one, for both are essential acts of a person giving himself to God. As in the Hebrew "Amen," the whole man believes.

In revelation a personal, loving God gives His innermost secrets to man, who through his faith can enter into the privacy of the transcendent God. Man, the person, believes the personal God, who reveals Himself to him. Faith is an interpersonal relationship between God and man similar to the personal exchange between a teacher and his student.[64]

Although the faith of Thomas Aquinas is not personal in the modern existential sense, nor does it stress the preconceptual intuition of the phenomenologists, it is, nevertheless, analogous to and compatible with today's developments in the theology of personal faith.

But is not Thomas' faith too intellectual? This was a criticism leveled by the Reformers. However, even a casual look at the act of faith as taught by Thomas reveals the importance of the affective power, for it is only at the command of the will that the intellect assents.[65] Perhaps an ecumenical bridge between the "affective" and more personal faith of the Reformers with its Augustinian background and the "intellectual" faith of

---

[62] The threefold *"credere"* illustrates well the inter-personal relationship of faith. *"Credo Deo,"* I believe the personal God, First Truth, revealing. *"Credo Deum,"* I believe Him as revealed. *"Credo in Deum,"* I believe in God, willingly assent to him. S.T., 2-2, q. 2, a. 2.

[63] S.T., 1, q. 1; 1-2, prol.; 2-2, q. 11.

[64] S.T., 2-2, q. 2, a. 3.

[65] 3S, d. 23, q. 2, a. 2, s. 1; D.V., q. 14, a. 1, 4; De Virt., a. 7; S.T., 2-2, q. 1, a. 4; q. 2, a. 1, ad 3.

Catholics with its Thomistic roots can be found in a correct interpretation of both Augustine and Aquinas. In the writings of each of these giants can be found the importance of both the affective and the intellectual powers in faith. Certainly both would agree that fundamentally it is the person who, using his faculties and cooperating with divine grace, believes God.

Finis

In conclusion, then, Thomas Aquinas teaches a dynamic faith, in which, drawn on by the interior invitation of the unseen First Truth, man gives a firm assent and at the same time strives restlessly to see Him. This basic dynamism, perfected by charity, a foretaste of beatitude, will never be satiated till man achieves the vision of and personal union with First Truth in eternal life, of which faith is the beginning and the anticipated possession.

The Death of God in
Karl Marx

DENIS DIRSCHERL, S.J.

There are few major political, religious, or social movements in history that have been able to survive and maintain the enthusiasm and fervor of their early years. Many, indeed, attacked in various ways from the outside or subjected to internal decay, eventually lost their vitality, disintegrated, and slipped from the memory of mankind. One of history's most colossal and world-shaking movements is now beginning to undergo the critical testing of its own inner fiber and strength. Soviet Russia, purported to be the showcase of international communism, despite external appearances to the contrary, is reaching the stage whereby most of those men who lived and had a hand in the revolutionary outbursts of 1917 and the following decade are now either dead or are no longer exerting a strong influence in the country's affairs.

As Soviet leaders themselves express it, they are now passing the political baton to the younger generation; it is up to the "sons" of Lenin, Stalin, and Khrushchev to preserve and further the historic thrust and mission of building communism. Whether this new breed will be able to instill fresh vigor into a system that has lost much of its early magnetism and dynamic appeal hinges on many variables both within and without the Soviet orbit. Chief among these many variables is the problem of God. The possibilities for maintaining and furthering the movement, or, on the contrary, the possibilities for fruitful confrontation, dialogue, and convergence with the West will depend on the courage and resourcefulness of this new breed's stance or approach to the life or death of God. Much too, of course, will depend on the creativity of the West in this same regard.

Mindful of the above momentous contingencies and exigencies of our contemporary situation vis-à-vis the Soviet Union and the West, this brief essay will attempt to synthesize and unify the ideas of the man most responsible for formulating the rationale for the death of God in the communist world view. As Isaiah Berlin has written, "No thinker in the nineteenth century has had so direct, deliberate and powerful an influence upon mankind as Karl Marx."[1] The difficulties of tying together this philosopher-revolutionary's ideas quickly become obvious to the interested individual. For Karl Marx's treatment of the existence of and belief in God, as contrasted with his economic works, is a very unsystematic one, obliging the inquirer to sift through many pages where relevant yet implicit references and nuances abound.

In his books and articles Marx sets down in no uncertain terms: (1) how belief in God began, (2) what metaphysical proof belief in such a Creator rests on, and (3) how this belief affects man. The further development of this scheme is the purpose of this essay. In it Marx and Engels are considered as one person — as two bodies with one soul. Indeed, in some sense, it would seem impossible to separate one partner's theory from the other. After their second meeting in 1844 in Paris "there is hardly a product of the one that was not edited or rewritten or at least debated with the other, and their correspondence fills several volumes."[2] Bober also concurs with this position, stating that "it would be impossible to dissever the thoughts of one from those of the other. Even if the task were possible, it is doubtful whether it would yield fruitful results."[3]

---

[1] Isaiah Berlin, *Karl Marx* (London, 1963), p. 1.

[2] Robert L. Heilbroner, *The Worldly Philosophers* (New York, 1953), p. 132.

[3] M. M. Bober, *Karl Marx's Interpretation of History* (Cambridge, 1950), p. viii.

A brief note on the early life of each of these philosophers will provide a helpful background. Marx's family history, both on his mother's and father's side, included a number of prominent rabbis, especially in the fifteenth and eighteenth centuries. Religion, however, meant little to Marx's parents, being, in the main, a mere convention for professional and commercial purposes. Though Heinrich Marx had the whole family adopt Christianity — Karl being baptized in 1824 — such an event was not disturbing, for this change had been taking place over many decades. Mehring says,

> the adoption of Christianity was an act of civilized progress for the freer spirits of Judaism, and the change of religion made by Heinrich Marx for himself and his family in 1824 must be understood in this sense and no other. It is possible that external circumstances determined the moment at which the change was made, but they were certainly not the cause.[4]

Though "little is known of his childhood and early years in Trier,"[5] the young Marx was an atheist from the beginning. Contrary to some biographies he apparently suffered from no religious crisis in his youth. "Neither in his voluminous correspondence nor in his books, did Karl Marx ever make any allusion to his supposed religious crisis, nor ever show any sympathy toward believers."[6] Calvez does find one isolated instance where the young Marx refers to a divinity who establishes an end for man; perfection for man and nature. As is evident from his writings, however, Marx revealed a special acquaintance with the Bible, especially the New Testament, and there are reports that he "often said that what pleased him most about the Christ of the Bible was his great love for children."[7]

Engels, on the other hand, came from a religious family strongly influenced by pietism of a rigidly authoritarian char-

[4] Franz Mehring, *Karl Marx* (London, 1951), p. 3.
[5] Berlin, *op. cit.*, p. 31.
[6] Ignace Lepp, *Atheism in Our Time* (New York, 1964), p. 58.
[7] Henri Chambre, *From Karl Marx to Mao Tse-tung* (New York, 1963), p. 16.

acter. He objected to its excesses and its failure to help the working class. Engels, more so than Marx, knew the fearful conditions under which the working class was gaining its sustenance. While helping to manage his father's factory in England under the partnership of Ermen and Engels, Frederick Engels took advantage of the opportunity to tour the country and to investigate the plight of the factory and mine workers. The result of this study was his book entitled *The Condition of the Working Class in England in 1844.* These experiences played a profound and dominant role in the life of this young businessman turned social scientist. By 1842 Engels was, according to his biographer, Gustav Mayer, already an atheist.

Both Marx's and Engels' position against God and religion was supported and strengthened by the onslaughts of the Young Hegelians: Bruno Bauer, Arnold Ruge, and Max Stirner. It was reserved for two other men, however, to set off the dramatic impulse for the rationale behind the death of God. David Strauss' *Life of Jesus,* which was published in 1835, provided the first impact. Strauss argued that the gospels were nothing but unconscious myths, legends created and supernaturalized by Jesus' disciples. More important still were two works from the pen of Ludwig Feuerbach, *The Essence of Christianity* which appeared in 1841, and *The Essence of Religion,* appearing in 1851. Both volumes made a telling, if not devastating, attack on traditional Christian concepts of God and religion.

Feuerbach's writings were so successful that even today he is considered by many to be the genius of atheistic philosophy of the nineteenth century. To understand Marx, then, it is necessary to understand Feuerbach. Thomas Masaryk, philosopher and historian, says that "anyone who has mastered these few pages on Feuerbach knows more of Marxism than he would from an undigested reading of the first volume of *Capital.*"[8] Fr. Sergius Bulgakov goes even further:

> I should like to endorse this judgment with redoubled emphasis: even a well-digested reading of all three volumes

---

[8] Gustav Wetter, *Dialectical Materialism* (New York, 1958), p. 14.

of *Capital* will give no such idea of the basic standpoint, the ruling spirit of Marxism, as familiarity with Feuerbach.[9]

Engels describes its effect on Marx and himself:

Then came Feuerbach's *Essence of Christianity*. With one blow it pulverized the contradiction, in that without circumlocutions it placed materialism on the throne again. . . . The spell was broken; the "system" was exploded and cast aside, and the contradiction, shown to exist only in our imagination, was dissolved. One must himself have experienced the liberating effect of this book to get an idea of it. Enthusiasm was general; we all became Feuerbachians.[10]

Feuerbach's self-appointed task was to prove that the distinction between the divine and the human was an illusion, to turn men from theologians into anthropologists. "Religion," he said, "is the dream of the human mind."[11] In this dream

Man denies as to himself only what he attributes to God. Religion abstracts from man, from the world; but it can only abstract from the limitations, from the phenomena; in short, from the negative, not from the essence, the positive, of the world and humanity: hence, in the very abstraction and negation it must recover that from which it abstracts, or believes itself to abstract. And thus, in reality, whatever religion consciously denies — always supposing that what is denied by it is something essential, true, and consequently incapable of being ultimately denied — it unconsciously restores in God. Thus, in religion man denies his reason; of himself he knows nothing of God, his thoughts are only worldly, earthly; he can only believe what God reveals to him.[12]

God, then, is the sum total of all the attributes of man in his most perfect form. Thus man's need for delimitization and

---

9 *Ibid.*, p. 14.

10 Marx and Engels, *Selected Works* (Moscow, 1958), II, pp. 367–368. (From Engel's "Ludwig Feuerbach and the End of Classical German Philosophy.")

11 Ludwig Feuerbach, *The Essence of Christianity* (New York, 1957), p. xxxix.

12 *Ibid.*, p. 27.

abstraction is governed and intensified in direct proportion to his own needs in life:

> The more empty life is, the fuller, the more concrete is God. The impoverishing of the real world and the enriching of God is one act. Only the poor man has a rich God. God springs out of a want; what man is in need of, whether this be a definite and therefore conscious, or an unconscious need — that is God. Thus the disconsolate feeling of a void, of loneliness, needed a God in whom there is society, a union of being fervently loving each other.[13]

Émile Saisset aptly summarizes the thrust of the above ideas in the 1840's: "Herr Feuerbach in Berlin, like Monsieur Comte in Paris, offers Christian Europe a new god to worship — the human race."[14] Feuerbach, indeed, is the spiritual father of Marxism.

In the preface to his dissertation entitled "On the Difference of Philosophy of Nature in Democritus and Epicurus" for his degree of Doctor of Philosophy at Jena in 1841, Marx used the confession of Prometheus to state his own position: "I hate all gods" — both of heavenly and human origin. Thus the condemnation of God and consequently of religion appears early in the works of Marx and Engels; its outright dismissal is strongly put forth in the *Manifesto*:

> But communism abolishes eternal truths, it abolishes all religion, and all morality, instead of constituting them on a new basis; it therefore acts in contradiction to all past historical experience.[15]

In a dramatic, and as is often their wont, polemical way, Marx and Engels characterize the necessity of reinterpreting man's origin, nature, and end in the opening lines of the *German Ideology* which appeared in 1846:

> Hitherto men have constantly made up for themselves false conceptions about themselves, about what they are

[13] *Ibid.*, p. 73.
[14] Henri De Lubac, *The Drama of Atheist Humanism* (New York, 1949), p. 77.
[15] Marx and Engels, *The Communist Manifesto* (New York, 1948), p. 29.

and what they ought to be. They have arranged their relationships according to their ideas of God, of normal Man, etc. The phantoms of their brains have gained the mastery over them. They, the creators, have bowed down before their creatures. Let us liberate them from the chimeras, the ideas, dogmas, imaginary being under the yoke of which they are pining away. Let us revolt against the rule of thoughts. Let us teach men, says one (Feuerbach), to exchange these imaginations for thoughts which correspond to the essence of man; says the second (Bruno Bauer), to take up a critical attitude to them; says the third (Max Stirner), to knock them out of their heads; and — existing reality will collapse.[16]

Even the once highly praised Feuerbach must step aside now for not penetrating to the actual depths of reality. For Feuerbach's basic critique, according to Marx and Engels, consisted in a call for man to change his thoughts. Put away the idea of the "God out there" and man will be on his way to solving all his problems. Not so say Marx and Engels.

Historically, Marx and Engels declare, men dreamed or invented false conceptions of themselves, about what their nature was and what they should be:

From the very early times when men, still completely ignorant of the structure of their own bodies, under the stimulus of dream apparitions came to believe that their thinking and sensation were not activities of their bodies, but of a distinct soul which inhabits the body and leaves it at death — from this time, men have been driven to reflect about the relation between this soul and the outside world. If in death it took leave of the body and lived on, there was no occasion to invent yet another distinct death for it. Thus arose the idea of its immortality which at that stage of development appeared not at all as a consolation but as a fate against which it was no use fighting, and often enough, as among the Greeks, as a positive misfortune. Not religious desire for consolation, but the quandary arising from the common universal ignorance of what to do with this soul (once its existence had been accepted)

---

[16] Marx and Engels, *The German Ideology* (London, 1940), p. 1.

after the death of the body — led in a general way to the tedious notion of personal immortality.[17]

From the most ancient times, then, man has been deceived by his own reflection.

In a similar fashion the first gods came into existence. The people of ancient history became mystified before nature and developed gods through the personification of nature.

> And these gods in the further development of religions assumed more and more an extramundane form, until finally by a process of abstraction, I might almost say of distillation, occurring naturally in the course of man's intellectual development, out of the more or less limited and mutually limiting gods there arose in the minds of men the idea of the one exclusive God of the monotheistic religions.[18]

God or religion, therefore, "is nothing but the fantastic reflection in men's minds of those external forces which control their daily life, a reflection in which the terrestrial forces assume the form of supernatural forces."[19] Thus man makes religion when he does not understand himself and the world about him, when he has lost his own image and identity or when he has not found it. The main task before man, therefore, is to destroy this illusion so that he can be really happy and become the man he should be. Man must ground his life in this world, establishing the truth of this world, not in some abstract unreality. For Marx, then, belief in God is non-rational, unreal; it is the worship of a myth.

When Marx approaches the very fundamental problem of God, however, he admits that the idea of a creation by a supreme being is difficult to remove from human consciousness:

> A man who lives by the grace of another regards himself as a dependent being. But I live completely by the grace of another if I owe him not only the sustenance of my life, but if he has, moreover, *created* my *life* — if he is

---

[17] Engels, *Ludwig Feuerbach (and the Outcome of Classical German Philosophy)*, (London, n.d.), p. 30.

[18] *Ibid.*, pp. 30–31.

[19] Engels, *Anti-Dühring* (New York, n.d.), p. 353.

the *source* of my life; and if it is not of my own creation, my life has necessarily a source of this kind outside it. The *Creation* is therefore an idea very difficult to dislodge from popular consciousness. The self-mediated being of nature and of man is *incomprehensible* to it, because it contradicts everything palpable in practical life.[20]

Regardless of the surface facility of this view or position, Marx says, it is a contradiction in terms:

> Now it is certainly easy to say to the single individual what Aristotle has already said. You have been begotten by your father and your mother; therefore in you the mating of two human beings — a species-act of human beings — has produced the human being. You see, therefore, that even physically, man owes his existence to man. Therefore you must not only keep sight of the *one* aspect — the *infinite* progression which leads you further to enquire: "Who begot my father? Who his grandfather?" etc. You must also hold on to the *circular movement* sensously perceptible in that progression, by which *man* repeats himself in procreation, thus always remaining the subject.[21]

But then we come to the question of infinite progression: Who created my father and my grandfather? And this problem continues all the way to infinity. But Marx says:

> You will reply, however: I grant you this circular movement; now grant me the progression which drives me ever further until I ask: Who begot the first man, and nature as a whole? I can only answer you: Your question is itself a product of abstraction. Ask yourself how you arrived at that question. Ask yourself whether your question is not posed from a standpoint to which I cannot reply, because it is a perverse one. Ask yourself whether that progression as such exists for a reasonable mind. When you ask about the creation of nature and man, you are abstracting, in so doing, from man and nature. You postulate them as *non-existent,* and yet you want me to prove them to you as *existing.*[22]

[20] Marx, *Economic and Philosophic Manuscripts of 1844* (Moscow, 1960), p. 112.
[21] *Ibid.*, pp. 112–113.
[22] *Ibid.*, p. 113.

Marx solves this difficulty by telling the individual to give up his abstraction:

> Now I say to you: Give up your abstraction and you will also give up your question. Or if you want to hold on to your abstraction, then be consistent, and if you think of man and nature as *non-existent*, then think of yourself as non-existent, for you too are surely nature and man. Don't think, don't ask me, for as soon as you think and ask, your *abstraction* from the existence of nature and man has no meaning. Or are you such an egoist that you postulate everything as nothing, and yet want yourself to be?[23]

Thus the existence of God as first cause ends in a dilemma, or as Professor Collins puts it so well, it

> involves a self-refuting process, which relieves one of the responsibility of providing an answer. The very problem of God's existence is impossible to pose, since it entails either the annihilation of the inquirer himself or the abandonment of the abstractive act and thus the silencing of the question about the first cause.[24]

Turning to another aspect of the death of God and religion, Engels says that the Catholic Church and Christianity in general have not only shown no concern for the masses but in fact were in some way a contributing cause to the division of classes:

> Christianity knew only *one* point in which all men were equal: that all were equally born in original sin — which corresponded perfectly with its character as the religion of the slaves and the oppressed. Apart from this it recognized, at most, the equality of the elect, which however was only stressed at the very beginning. The traces of common ownership which were also found in the early stages of the new religion can be ascribed to the solidarity of a prescribed sect rather than to real equalitarian ideas. Within a very short time the establishment of the distinction between priests and laymen put an end even to this tendency to Christian equality.[25]

---

23 *Ibid.*
24 James Collins, *God in Modern Philosophy* (Chicago, 1959), p. 252.
25 Engels, *Anti-Dühring*, pp. 119–120.

Furthermore, Marx says, "the social principles of Christianity preach the necessity of a ruling and an oppressed class, and all they have for the latter is the pious wish the former will be charitable."[26] These same "social principles of Christianity justified the slavery of antiquity, glorified the serfdom of the Middle Ages, and equally know, when necessary, how to defend the oppression of the proletariat, although they make a pitiful face over it."[27] Summarily, belief in the existence of God and the profession of religion, especially for the proletariat class, force man to stay in his own wretched place in society.

Becoming more specific on what he considers Christianity's perpetration of class division, Marx draws a corollary from economic exploitation where he says that every imperfection of man "is a bond with heaven — an avenue giving the priest access to his heart,"[28] i.e., to the detriment of the individual concerned. Marx expands on this idea by drawing from a piece of literature current in his own day. His intent, it seems, is to set forth this fictional account as being representative of priestly counseling, guidance which results in confusion and frustration:

> *Fleur de Maria* already finds it wrong that she took a new happy situation in life simply for what it *really was*, that she felt it as a new happiness, that her attitude to it was a natural, not a supernatural one. She accuses herself of seeing in the man who saved her what he *really* was, her saviour, instead of supposing some imaginary saviour, *God*, in his place. She is already caught in religious hypocrisy which takes away from *another man* what he has deserved in respect of men in order to give it to God and which considers anything and everything human in man as alien to God and everything inhuman in him as *really* God's own.[29]

In a similar vein Marx states that "the classical saint of Christianity mortified *his* body for the salvation of the souls

[26] Marx and Engels, *Basic Writings on Politics and Philosophy*, edited by Lewis S. Feuer (New York, 1959), p. 268. (From Marx: "The Communism of the Paper *Rheinischer Beobachter*".)
[27] *Ibid.*, p. 268.
[28] Marx, *Economic*, p. 116.
[29] Marx and Engels, *The Holy Family* (Moscow, 1956), p. 231.

of the masses; the modern, educated saint mortifies *the bodies of the masses* for the salvation of his own soul."[30] Moving closer to the core critique of belief in God and religion, Marx says:

> The social principles of Christianity declare all vile acts of the oppressors against the oppressed to be either the just punishment of original sin and other sins or trials that the Lord in his infinite wisdom imposes on those redeemed. The social principles of Christianity preach cowardice, self-contempt, abasement, submission, humility, in a word all the qualities of the *canaille;* and the proletariat, not wishing to be treated as *canaille,* needs its courage, its self-esteem, its pride, and its sense of independence more than its bread.[31]

Another aspect of this same phenomenon, Marx feels, reveals itself from the halo of holiness which motivates the "canaille" to put up with this rough, un-Christian treatment:

> Indeed, holy missions are always bound up with the holy beings who pursue them; for such missions are of a purely idealistic nature and have their being only in the head of the person concerned. All idealists, philosophic and religious, ancient and modern, believe in inspirations, in revelations, saviors, miracle-workers; whether their belief takes a crude religious, or a polished philosophic, form depends only upon their cultural level, just as the degree of energy which they possess, their character, their social position, etc., determine whether their attitude to a belief in miracles is a passive or an active one, i.e., whether they enthral their flock by working miracles or whether they are themselves the sheep who are enthralled; they further determine whether the aims to be pursued are practical or merely theoretical.[32]

In its essence, Marx declares,

> religion is the sigh of the oppressed creature, the heart of a heartless world, just as it is the spirit of an unspiritual

---

[30] Marx and Engels, *On Religion* (Moscow, 1957), p. 127. ("Anti-Church Movement — Demonstration in Hyde Park" in London, June 25, 1855).

[31] Marx and Engels, *Basic Writings . . .* , pp. 268–269.

[32] Marx and Engels, *The German Ideology,* p. 181.

situation. It is the *opium* of the people . . . is only the illusory sun, which revolves around man as long as he does
not revolve around himself.[33]

In the same context, and while reacting against Hegel's philosophy, Marx says that

man is no abstract being, squatting outside the world.
Man is *the world of man*, the state, society. This state,
this society produce religion, a *perverted world consciousness*, because they are a *perverted world*. . . . The
struggle against religion is therefore mediately the fight
against *the other world*, of which religion is the spiritual
aroma."[34]

Marx's critique of religion culminates in "the death of God."
Therein lies the road to man's happiness:

The abolition of religion as the *illusory* happiness of the
people is required for their *real* happiness. The demand to
give up the illusions about its condition is the *demand to
give up a condition which needs illusions*. The criticism
of religion is therefore *in embryo the criticism of the vale
of woe*, the *halo* of which is religion. . . . *The task of
history*, therefore, once the *world beyond the truth* has disappeared, is to establish the *truth of this world*. The *immediate task of philosophy*, which is at the service of history, once the *saintly form* of human self-alienation has
been unmasked, is to unmask self-alienation in its *unholy
forms*. Thus the criticism of heaven turns into the criticism
of the earth, the *criticism of religion into the criticism of
right*, and the *criticism of theology* into the *criticism of
politics*. . . .[35]

In other words, Marx's view is that religious belief teaches
man to be passive, to suppress his own will, to put down
"temptations" to rise up against his oppressors, to cede to another man what is rightfully his own. Thus man is dehuman-
ized by attributing to God and the oppressors what really belongs to himself. "The more man puts into God, the less he

[33] Marx and Engels, *Basic Writings* . . . , p. 263. ("Toward the Critique
of Hegel's Philosophy of Right".)
[34] Marx and Engels, *Basic Writings* . . . , pp. 262–263.
[35] *Ibid.*, p. 263.

retains in himself."[36] In effect man will believe in God only in the proportion that he lacks the courage to stand up for himself, to be a man. Where the rich are taught their rights, the poor are educated in their duties to the ruling class, to aid their further exploitation. Thus initiative to better man's own existence is destroyed. Such beliefs breed false hopes and deliver false promises, while at the same time making man live in two worlds; as a result, conflicts develop which man cannot solve. In a word, God, Christianity, and religion are dead once man wakes up to the fact that the exploiters are foisting God and religion on him to maintain the social and political status quo.

Besides stating that belief in God, a human soul, and an after-life all arose from the "mystification of nature," that the proof for the existence of God is mere "abstraction," and that those who believe in Christianity have oppressed their fellow men, Marx puts forth another reason for the overthrow of God. A major reason why religion and a belief in God have such a strong influence on the masses, according to Marx, is that the oppressed are confused, cut off from the world of reality, their work and fellow man; in a word they are alienated. "*Religious* distress is at the same time the *expression* of real distress and the *protest* against real distress."[37] Since man is alienated in the social and political areas of his life and unable to fulfill his proper needs, he finds refuge by seeking compensation in another world that does not exist. As Marx's friend, the poet Heine, wrote: "Heaven was invented for the use of men for whom the earth offered nothing."[38] Man projects himself into a false and unreal heaven where he is promised everything so that he will patiently suffer the shortcomings of the real, concrete world. The religion of a "heaven" is an instrument to defend unjust government by promising the exploited classes something they will never receive. But even these promises do not solve man's alienation; on the contrary, the alienation is compounded:

[36] Marx, *Economic* . . . , p. 70.
[37] Marx and Engels, *Basic Writings* . . . , p. 263.
[38] Lepp, *Atheism in Our Time,* p. 64.

The essential character of religious experience, of the religious mode of existence, actually appeared to Marx as religious wretchedness. The religious man does not know himself to be so secure; on the contrary he is a much troubled person. He comes face to face with the Infinite, he confronts God, who creates, judges, condemns, and destroys. The attitude of the creature before the Creator, humility, consists in states of abjection, of separation from oneself (alienation), of the radical loss of oneself. Religion places man in a Paradise, granted, but within religion (in the projected world), man's being is found once more in a state of wretchedness, which gains nothing becoming "other-worldly."[39]

Yet man has no other recourse but to turn to another world. As a result, the belief in God, the resignation to man's own fate becomes a vampire, to use the words of Feuerbach, a vampire that thrives on the flesh and blood of man.

According to Marx, then, man is the supreme being, and nature is entirely self-sustaining. Consequently there is no practical need of God. God is dead. Inquiring about God only dehumanizes man; it makes man a stranger to himself by bowing down to religion, a sick product of an unreal world. By dethroning God and religion, man can get behind the facade of man's alienation and thereby reconcile himself to nature and reality. Rather than wasting time on attacking God and religion, however, Engels counsels that man have courage and faith in history of which he is the primary collaborator. From here nature will take its rightful course:

When society, by taking possession of all means of production and using them on a planned basis, has freed itself and all its members from the bondage in which they are now held by these means of production which they themselves have produced but which now confront them as an irresistible extraneous force; when therefore man no longer merely proposes, but also disposes — only then will the last extraneous force which is still reflected in religion vanish; and with it will also vanish the religious reflection itself, for

---

[39] Jean-Yves Calvez, *La Pensée de Karl Marx* (Paris, 1956), p. 89.

the simple reason that then there will be nothing left to reflect.[40]

In the last analysis, man must put away thoughts about God and devote an all-out effort and concentration to the present situation of this real concrete world. Atheism, the first and indispensible step in healing man's alienation, paves the way for breaking the political, social, and above all, the economic bonds of alienation. Atheism, the motto of the Young Hegelians, was only the beginning of the full-blown Marxian critique, a critique that proposed to give man a plan to work out his problems and suffering in this world.

A Brief Rejoinder

Two wise historians, John and Barbara Hammond, made a remarkable observation in the first decades of this century. They pointed out that the more closely we study a period of history, the more clearly it appears that the errors and troubles of that particular age are due to a false spirit — an unfortunate fashion in men's ways of thinking and emotional response, a tendency to be overwhelmed by the phenomena of the times. Absorbed in the spirit of the times, lacking in fresh perspectives, men often are unable to distinguish the possible from the impossible. Unable to detach themselves from the situation, they come to think it is their business merely to explain, rather than to control the forces of the hour.

This all too often human failing of being overwhelmed by the times certainly could not be attributed to Marx. Indeed the promotion of the idea of changing the world is one of his strongest positive characteristics. One of his theses against Feuerbach epitomizes this idea: "The philosophers have only *interpreted* the world, in various ways; the point, however, is to change it."[41] His words and writings were by no means mere flailings in the air. Being a critical philosopher, he meant to expose the old world for all its brutality and inhumanity, offering his interpretation and his plan for transforming society as a way out of the apparent impasse of the early and middle nineteenth

---

[40] Engels, *Anti-Dühring*, p. 355.
[41] Marx and Engels, *Basic Writings* . . . , p. 245.

century. Marx advocated action, and his

action was given specificity in a radical new emphasis on *work*. Man becomes man, becomes alive through work, for through work man loses his isolation and becomes a social or co-operative being, and thus learns of himself; and through work he is able to transform nature as well.[42]

Marx's own life, especially while in England, was a tribute to his theoretical efforts:

His mode of living consisted of daily visits to the British Museum reading-room, where he normally remained from nine in the morning until it closed at seven; this was followed by long hours of work at night, accompanied by ceaseless smoking, which from a luxury had become an indispensable anodyne; this affected his health permanently and he became liable to frequent attacks of a disease of the liver sometimes accompanied by boils and an inflamation of the eyes, which interfered with his work, exhausted and irritated him, and interrupted his never certain means of livelihood.[43]

Ultimately, for Marx, man resolves and finds himself in meaningful work, under human conditions. Religion or belief in God, on the other hand, is a sign and symbol of human alienation. This latter idea is the unifying theme of this little essay, and its spirit runs through, no matter how subtle and implicit, all of Marx's and Engel's early works: *Condition of the Working Class in England in 1844* (1844), *Economic and Philosophic Manuscripts of 1844* (1844), *Holy Family* (1845), *German Ideology* (1846), *Poverty of Philosophy* (1847), and *Communist Manifesto* (1848).

In such a short treatment of Marx's ideas on God and religion there is always the danger of distortion through isolation of a topic to which Marx himself never devoted a complete or systematic treatise. In this sense, all the above ideas must be understood in all the complex political, social, economical, and religious conditions of nineteenth century Europe. Included also, of course, would be all the "big men" of the day, men like Darwin, Feuerbach, Hegel, Mill, Owen, Proudhon, Ricardo,

---

[42] Leopold Labedz, ed., *Revisionism* (London, 1962), p. 199.
[43] Berlin, *op. cit.,* p. 195.

Saint-Simon, Strauss, etc. All these men in one way or another had an important part to play in the formulation of Marx's thought. To understand the Russian scene of the same period men like Bakunin, Chernyshevsky, and Nechaev, among others, would also have to be considered.

By way of a short conclusion we can safely say that Marx's atheism, his anti-theistic philosophy is an intrinsic part of his entire world view. There is no way of denying this fact in face of all the evidence from his writings. Besides the many citations to this effect there are also the choice words Marx reserves for those hostile to his ideas: "religious minds," "crypto-believers in God," and "theologians."

The problem still remaining is that one may naturally enough become open to Marx's world view once he admits or holds that God does not exist. In that case, to paraphrase Dostoevsky, if God does not exist, all things become possible and legitimate. In this context and in its historical origin, and it might be added, in some sections of the globe today, this same type of "conversion" has and is still taking place. The Marxian philosophy may be taken as so much nonsense within the Christian context. As a matter of fact, though, it has much to tell Christians of the past and present century. And for all its flaws, even some of its brutal principles, it has made a good deal of sense to more than a smattering of people outside Christianity.

However successful or unsuccessful today's forces using or claiming to use this philosophical system may be, Marx, for sure, was too eager and willing to accept the heavily polemical propositions of his fellow philosophers: Bauer, Hegel, Ruge, Stirner, Strauss, and most of all, Feuerbach. As Lepp points out, these men "simply helped him motivate and formulate rationally his revolt against the gods, especially against the Christian God. . . ."[44] Marx's remarks on the subject, Collins notes,

are intended as mere footnotes to the main text, as a postscript to a critique already achieved in its main points by his predecessor. Marx does not experience any need for a fresh appraisal of God and the religious attitude, since

[44] Lepp, *op. cit.*, p. 60.

he accepts as almost definitive the exposition and criticism
made by Feuerbach. The limiting influence of this special
historical situation upon the validity of Marx's atheistic position can be measured by examining his views on the proofs
of God's existence and religious alienation.[45]

Lepp makes a similar observation:

> What is interesting in these and similar tirades is that
> Marx, the man of science, feels no obligation to verify or
> justify anything he says about religion. He would not have
> allowed himself to criticize the economic laws and princi-
> ples of his time by basing his remarks solely on the super-
> ficial observation of a given factory owner in Manchester;
> he carefully studied the writings of Adam Smith, Ricardo,
> and the other approved theoreticians of capitalism. He did
> nothing of the sort in the matter of religion. What he called
> the "social principles of Christianity" could obviously be
> found in the behavior of certain Christians and perhaps in
> some sermons, but he would have sought in vain for any
> confirmation of such principles in any theological writing
> or papal document. This fully confirms our conviction that
> Marx's atheism is completely unscientific. It relates to a
> complex emotional situation, and must be explained by
> depth psychology rather than by political economy.[46]

Lepp's studies in depth psychology reveal that Marx's atheism
is largely in the area of psychological and emotional motivation. "It is indisputable," he says,

> that the founder of Communism did not become an atheist
> as a result of his philosophical or scientific studies, nor as
> a result of his political and social battles against the con-
> servative and reactionary churches. In light of the facts,
> it can be maintained with much more truth that it was,
> rather, Marx's ferocious atheism which played an important
> role in his political and philosophical formation.[47]

To a large extent Marx's analysis of religion and belief in
God arose from his own concrete set of circumstances in the
Prussian state of his day:

[45] Collins, *op. cit.*, pp. 250–251.
[46] Lepp, *op. cit.*, pp. 66–67.
[47] *Ibid.*, p. 57.

The Europe of their day was scarcely Christian in the religious sense, although it continued to be so sociologically. In their search for social identity the Jewish intellectuals were continually coming up against barriers that were erected in the name of religion. Consciously, they fought against "religious alienation" in the name of philosophy, science, or history. Unconsciously, they fought against a Christianity whose adherents set them apart and obliged them to feel like strangers in their own homeland. Resentment plays an important role in the atheism of almost all the Jews I know, and in the atheism of Karl Marx its role is probably unusually dominant.[48]

Obviously enough, the non-acceptance of one metaphysical proof for the existence of God, as indicated in the manuscripts of 1844, does not end the question of God's existence. Besides, there are other philosophical formulations. Faith must be adequately considered also. Then, too, belief in God and the practice of religion in themselves alone are hardly meant to solve all man's problems; man must do his share. Here Marx himself, in some sense an existentialist, once again points to the value and importance of labor, that purposeful work and constructive human effort might eliminate much useless strife and suffering in our all too often inhuman world. Marx saw the inherent weakness of one aspect of mankind, and Chambre describes it accurately. "The human heart is something strange, especially when carried about in a wallet." Finally, Marx could have served his fellow men mightily by directing his passionate commitment and fury toward contributing positive formulations on right reason for a better world. Instead, he chose to proclaim the dirge of God and the need for destroying society. But, as Barbara Ward indicates, "religion is not abolished by the 'abolition' of God; the religion of Caesar takes its place."

[48] *Ibid.*, pp. 58–59.

The Church and Contemporary Atheism

J. MARTIN POSADAS, S.J.

No reflection upon the present condition of man can be complete without a consideration of the current attitude of forgetfulness of God or displacement of God which we call atheism. The world today lives outside the Church and outside God. More than half the population of the world has adopted, and very seriously, a philosophico-political system which is expressly atheistic. Many other peoples still build temples and churches, and still mention the name of God, but their real lives proceed as if He were not there. All churches deplore this situation; non-church people accept it either enthusiastically or matter-of-factly, but nobody denies it as a fact.

To speak about atheism in the twentieth century is to speak of something that has many facets, many manifestations, something that is ambivalent and ambiguous. Rather than undertake the task of dissecting it in its different components and different types, I believe that, for my purpose here, it will be better to take it as a whole, in all its complexity and ambiguity. My intention in this essay is merely to make some observations on the encounter between today's atheism and today's church. Therefore I believe it is better to take atheism historically, not analytically.

Yet there is one specification that I would like to make for the

CHURCH AND CONTEMPORARY ATHEISM

sake of clarity. Of all the facets of contemporary atheism there
is one that I will exclude. It is the atheism for ethical reasons,
the one provoked by the scandal of evil. This type of atheism
flourished mainly after the war, when wounds were still open
and men were understandably shocked at the spectacle of what
men could do to each other. It was the reaction to the tears of
the children and the suffering of the innocent. Grace, God, and
heaven were rejected as poor substitutes for this flagrant absence
of justice. This was the atheism represented by Camus in *The
Stranger*. But this atheism is almost gone because, although today we live in greater justice, we certainly live in greater abundance and comfort, and this is quite often a narcotic of moral
sensibility. I personally have more sympathy for this type of
atheism than for any other, yet I will not speak of it, if for no
other reason than that it is not *the* representative form of atheism in the modern world.

I will deal with the other atheism of this century, the more
optimistic and self-confident atheism of technological progress
and scientific advancement. When I talk about contemporary
atheism I am referring to this phenomenon.

Contemporary atheism is not aristocratic, as was the atheism
proposed by Nietzsche's superman; nor is it a rational conclusion
arrived at after a highly speculative process, as was the atheism
of the Enlightenment. It belongs to everybody, high and low,
and it is not a conclusion but, quite the opposite, a starting
point. Contemporary atheism feels absolutely no internal need
to provide a logical justification for its exclusion of God. Atheism
today feels "in possession"; if something has to be proved and
justified, it is the existence of God. And this has not been done
to today's atheist's satisfaction. Besides the atheist *today* does
not talk in a language of metaphysics; he finds his justification
either in history or in his own results and success.

Today's atheism is basically a system of values which puts
man at the center, origin, and apex of all values, and consequently finds no place for God. The system is complete without God. There is no violent denial of Him, no argument, no
discussion about the point: God is just not there.

Man today creates his own world. By the mastery of the sciences, industry, and technology, man gives shape and form to the world of nature that surrounds him. He no longer lives in a given surrounding; he makes it and transforms it. Just as prehistoric men one day realized that instead of having to look for a hole in the rocks to live in, they could build themselves a home wherever they pleased, so men today feel that they do not have to accommodate passively to their environment any more because they can build it, all of it, just as they please. Man is the creator of the cosmos he lives in. What is not yet touched by him is chaos, is pre-creation, until the day — not so distant — in which he will lay hands on it.

Man today also believes that he is master of his own self. He is his own ruler and there is no other ruler of mankind. Certain eugenic practices, psychoanalysis, birth-control and massive propaganda are some ways in which this is exercised.

Man today also feels that he is his own redeemer, his own Prometheus. Mankind's concrete experience of its capabilities of autoredemption, of a salvation of man by man, makes the image of God recede and vanish. Does God exist? It does not matter; to discuss the matter would be a loss of the precious time man has to construct his world. Man has nothing to expect from a God to whom he prayed so much in past centuries without ever being heard. The faithful could once kneel and pray and offer sacrifices; their God has inexorably let them die of cold, of hunger, of epidemics. If life is now, for an increasing number of men, more liveable, more human, this is due to man's own efforts and not to God's intervention. Whatever man was led to pray for formerly, he can achieve now by himself.

Finally, man feels that there is no supra-mundane providence, but he himself is his own providence. He has his own plan and his own goals. Whatever happens in history is his doing, his decision, and a supra-mundane providence can only be invented later to sanction what man has already decided and done. The only real orientation that history and the world have is the one that depends on man's decisions.

The believer in general and the Church in particular are

confronted with this historical state of things, with this civilization of men without God. These two entities — let us simplify them into two names: atheism and church — are facing each other. What will come out of this confrontation? War or diplomatic compromise? Gradual absorption of one by the other? Mutual influence? We do not know. But we can speculate on some aspect of what it should be.

The Church finds herself in front of this world, enveloped by it, and called to be in it — and not elsewhere — a living witness to the crucified and risen Lord, and to make redemption present and operative in it. This may not be the situation some have dreamed of, but this is the situation in which we all find ourselves. Some time ago this confrontation was thought of with secret fear and open aversion. It was thought of as an irreconcilable incompatibility. Atheism was proclaimed as an impossibility; godlessness could only be explained as obstinate bad will and human progress that had borne it was to be condemned. This thinking is fortunately dépassé. Contemporary theology has tackled the problem with considerably more serenity and a more lucid charity. Several lines of thought have developed in this direction, all of which, obviously, I cannot describe at length. But still I would like to say a few words about them. One of these relatively recent developments in theological thinking on the problems of atheism turns about the axis of unbelief, the necessity of faith for salvation, and the universal salvific will of God. The theologians have tried to combine successfully these three elements, giving pre-eminence to the latter. But the whole treatment seems to me relatively academic. I prefer a more pastoral view (and I use the term pastoral in the sense Vatican II used it when it described itself as a pastoral Council). The belief that all those who do not have explicit faith are not saved, or, on the contrary, that they are, may make us more educated theologically — and this is a very good thing — but does not change the number of those who are saved or the way in which de facto they are saved.

This position, especially in its more benevolent exponents like Fr. Congar, has another facet which is also a bit disconcerting inasmuch as it does not treat the problem seriously enough. They say: when a man is wholeheartedly committed to a sublime cause, like human progress, civilization, justice, he is not really an atheist because he finds the absolute in that great cause to which he is committed. I really do not think that we should never take the atheist at his word. I would like to quote Roger Vaillant on this:

> For a Catholic nothing worthwhile can be foreign to God. If an honorable man is an atheist it is because he seeks God and to seek God is already to have found Him. If he protests that he does not seek God, then that is because he seeks Him without knowing it: Providence has hidden ways. . . . God is a vicious circle from which we cannot escape. . . . The truth is, it is impossible to argue with a Catholic.

There is quite a bit of evidence — as we saw before — that men can be quite radically atheist, existentially removed from God and with no necessity or desire to look for Him. There can be, of course, instances of implicit belief of the unbeliever; and I am convinced it is true that grace is more widely accepted than is recorded in the Church's statistics. Nevertheless, we cannot legitimately establish as a starting point for a consideration of this historical atheism that all unbelievers believe in spite of themselves.

There is still another trend in the theological treatment of this problem, the one which could be called more pastoral. I have chosen to treat my subject following this type of thinking because I consider that in it theology can be at its best because it can be in its place. Theology is a reflection intimately related and subordinated to the ecclesial experience. The horizon of theology is the Church's horizon; not less, but nothing more either. Insofar as theology considers of second order the pastoral mission of the Church, theology loses all meaning, and this desertion engenders in the Church a tendency either to abandon the essential issues and tasks and take refuge in the security of anodyne practices, or, in the other extreme, to venture recklessly in very imaginative innovations that are equally feeble and hide no less the true originality of the Gospel. Theology has been responsible for both excesses when it has abandoned its nature of ecclesial reflection. With this in mind — and turning back to our subject — this type of theological thinking tries to understand for itself the historical situation of the godless society, and tries to make a sincere evaluation of it in a pastoral scale of values.

Today's historical moment is the God-given situation in which the Christian has to live his Christian life and in which the Church has to preach the Christian message. The salvific action of Christ is eternal; the moral message of the Gospels is for all ages, for all men. Therefore the Church has definitely something to give to this age of ours. It is necessary to postulate a certain theological realism and avoid any dreams of a supposedly better situation. The Church has to be and to act in the real situation in which she finds herself, without postponing anything for a fictitious ideal situation. The Christian cannot be, as Giono describes him, "the fellow who walks across the battlefield with a flower in his hand," that is to say, alien to all that mankind is doing and undergoing, abstracted in his own unreal microcosmos. The Church cannot close in upon herself either, forming a ghetto, a sort of reservation for the elect, living (or dying?) in their own little world, speaking an archaic dialect incomprehensible to everybody else, and conducting their affairs in a style that can only be considered by the outsider as a well-preserved piece of folklore.

On the subject of atheism, Pascal wrote: "Atheism is an indication of spiritual vigor . . . but only to a certain degree." This is quite true and could very well be taken by the Church as a basis for her attitude in this matter. Atheism, especially the one I am talking about, has a certain undeniable value; it also has an area of barrenness, of insufficiency, as Pascal noted. Atheism has a value but not precisely as atheism, not precisely as denial of God, not in its chemically pure state. But this is the point: contemporary atheism does not present itself as chemically pure in a vacuum but as an element of the historical existential situa-

tion of today. Although basic, it is still one element among
many of the scientific and technological era.

Let us examine some aspects of value in contemporary atheism
and also indicate its insufficiency and how the Church has all
that in which today's atheism falls short, all that which is
needed to vivify fully the history of man today.

In the first place, today's atheist shows an undeniable courage
to build this world. There is a value here. Man, through his
own ingenuity and tenacity, has found a way to dominate the
forces of nature and to make them work for him. He has discovered to his own astonishment and delight the secrets of the
microcosmos, and is well on his way toward the discovery of
the macrocosmos. He is no longer totally at the mercy of the
forces of nature, but by science and technology he channels their
momentum for his own benefit. Every new discovery in science
or development in technology provides more tools for further
progress. Human labor has become less of a servitude and has
acquired a more creative nature. Man is also engaged in manag-
ing his political relations, in the international and national
sphere, in an effort to make them more rational, less subject to
blind impulses and narrowmindedness, and thus give a stable
structure to his society. All this is thought without God and
done without Him.

It should be obvious by now that in this last paragraph I have
borrowed the words not of the historians but of the most optimistic panegyrists of our twentieth century, and that reality does
not quite match this rather triumphal description. But still, for
all its shortcomings, there is something of unquestionable value
here, both in the effort and in the achievements. This process
of human progress is good and has to be recognized as such. It
cannot be denied because it is godless. On the contrary it has
to be completed and vivified with what it lacks. Atheism does
not necessarily follow from the real values of human progress;
God has to be brought into this process, not against it. The
Church has to vivify this movement of human progress with the
idea of Genesis. Man is created to the image and likeness of God.
He is given the ability and the responsibility to grow and to dom-

inate the earth and all that is in it. In doing so, he becomes more and more the image of God. who is master and creator of all things. In the words of Irenaeus of Lyons, *"gloria Dei, vivens homo,"* man, with all his realizations, is a shining forth of the glory of God, and it will be more and more so, the more man dominates and molds the earth. It is precisely the Church's teaching of the radical created nature of the world as the material given to man's industry and work that legitimates the will to conquer it. More than any humanistic self-asserting and God-denying creed, it is that Christian teaching on freedom and absolute responsibility, trusting to man's hands not only his worldly existence but his eternal existence as well, that makes man true master of his destiny. Conceding all this to man does not take anything away from God. The task of vivification that the Church has confronted with modern man is, on the other hand, to tell him that it does not take anything away from man to recognize God as his creator.

There is a second element in the configuration of contemporary secular civilization which is of value, and which also needs a vivification and rectification that Christianity alone can give it.

The Promethean man of today feels an almost violent thrust to the future. He feels that his mastery over the cosmos is just beginning, that the possibilities and the work to be done are immense. There is a constant reference to tomorrow: man of tomorrow, the world of tomorrow, the city of tomorrow, etc. This is constantly present in all areas of thought and it is not just a mirage, a vague hope. It is the realization of a verifiable movement forward, and, specially, the realization that the necessary tools are there and the determination is not lacking. Each new human achievement invigorates this thrust to the future, a future which is envisioned as overflowing in abundance, in justice, and in happiness for all men. This attitude provides modern man with a very concrete image of self-made eschatology, be it the Soviet paradise, the Great Society or whatever other names he may give to his *"saeculum venturum,"* to his promised land.

This dynamism to the future has to be vivified too and channeled toward the only possible satisfactory termination: eternity.

Left to its own, this dynamism, which is a value, can easily be diverted and spend its real self in banalities, in pragmatism, the cult of usefulness, or in mere materialism, the cult of comfort and security. Kept in its generous vigor, it raises man above himself to an absolute value beyond this world, to an Absolute that is not made by man. Christianity has always been the religion of an infinite future; no matter how ambiguous, insufficient and materialistic it may be, either as a complete catastrophe or as totally alien to Christianity itself. The Church can vivify this movement, first, by giving moral responsibility before God to the legitimate will concerned with a future within this world, to be created by man himself; second, by giving to this will the openness toward God's infinite life which is, in the most proper and true sense, our future.

Modern theologians have also realized that this atheistic configuration of the world today has — indirectly, of course — a certain influence in the internal life of the Church. Atheism — and today's atheism much more than the atheism of the nineteenth century — is an agent of purification of the faith of the believer. By this I do not pretend to imply that atheism is a good thing. Recognition that the devil occasionally helps to build has never meant that the devil was not the devil but an angel in disguise, whose disciples we could cheerfully become. Yet he does indirectly help to build.

The Christian has to live today in a pluralistic society. The actual configuration of modern life is far from being traced over the patterns of the Church's life. The Christian of another age may have found protection for his faith in the public recognition of God by the state, and support for his morality in the accepted customs of everyday life. This historical influence of the Church in peoples' lives may have been so universal that to be a Christian might have seemed just being like everyone else. This is not so in our days, and I feel that it hasn't been so for quite some time. In today's world, created outside God, Christianity cannot expect to receive any significant support from institutional morality, custom, public opinion, or even normal conformism. In today's world there are no more Christian countries. To a large and increasing extent, there are no more Christian families where faith is handed down and accepted together with the family name, the family trade, and the family fortune. The advantages and disadvantages of the old and new situation can be weighed to no end. But this is a fact here to stay, and it has a definite influence on the attitude of belief, in the existential way in which the Christian goes about his faith. Faith today is more and more a personally discovered and freely elicited decision, not induced or maintained by any social pressure or force of habit, but by a personal commitment. True faith and adherence to the Church, in any age, was and must have been a free decision of the individual. But now if it is not this, it is nothing; and this is good because at least it does not look like faith. There are no disguises, no misunderstandings, no pretensions. This is a salutary ascesis, historically imposed, that emphasizes and shows the value of what is really fundamental. The Church is obliged to change from a Church of masses to a Church of individuals. From all this the eternal truth is emphasized, namely, that Christian life is always the fulfillment of a unique personal individuality and that it cannot merely rest in the following of practices and external obedience to laws and discipline. The Church cannot count on external and collective patterns of life to produce or maintain a living faith. Now that the world makes them to a large extent impossible, she is forced to rely on something else, on something that, in the end, turns out to be more reliable.

From this also follows that if the Church cannot rely on external practices and habits of everyday life because these have become secular and a-religious, and if she has to count largely on the free decision of each individual, she cannot pretend to operate efficiently with a double standard, forcing the individual in intra-ecclesial matters to be guided totally by rules and structures, with little room for personal decisions. The Church will gradually depart from a system that intends to carry the Christian on rollers, a structure that does everything for him, tells him what to believe, what to do and what not to do in every instance, what to think and what kind of thoughts to treat as temptations, how to behave, how to make the right responses. It also follows that the Church will not put as much emphasis on uniformity as if this were unity, or in inducing an external objective good conduct as if this were the conversion of the heart she wishes to bring forth.

In all these ways, very indirectly if you want, but yet perceptibly, this technological civilization that does not mention God's name, has an impact in the internal life of the Church.

There is a second beneficial impact — also indirect and paradoxical — that today's atheistic society induces in the Church. Society, civilization, the state, have taken — and quite seriously — the responsibility of caring for the sick, feeding the hungry, educating the illiterate, developing the underdeveloped areas, and in general of alleviating human misery. They never believed that human goodness was an exclusive prerogative of the clergy or of Church-directed organizations. They have become competitors of the Church in this endeavor, and they have the means to do much more than all the Church-inspired charities put together. Whether from a motive of human goodness or simply of order, hygiene and efficiency, the fact is that one day — they claim — there will be no place for the good Samaritan because the state will take care of all the injured at the side of the road. All this is done in the name of no God.

This, which is a historical fact already here, or to come very soon, will contribute to a reappraisal on the part of the Church of her own nature as an institution of supernatural salvation. This element will have to stand out among all others. The Church as such does not have the same mission and responsibility that the individual Christians have; or, putting it the other way around, the individual Christians have a responsibility and a mission which the Church as such does not have. The Christian has the responsibility to work side by side with all his brothers of good will — believer or not — in the alleviation of human misery and human suffering, and in the effort of building a better world for all men. He is better endowed to do it than his non-believing brother because he has a higher motivation, Christian charity, and a moral guideline of supernatural wisdom, the Gospels. But, like his non-believing brother, the Christian has no formula of how the city of men has to be: he has to experiment, he has to seek, he has to probe, in anxiety and hope. All this the Christian does in his civilization, together with all men of good will, without any need of duplicating in a Christian version all that his non-believing brother is doing in his own secular way.

But the Church, as Church, does not have this mission. Her mission is not to build the city of men but the city of God, her mission is to mediate a salvation which is to be definitive in the life to come and is inchoate in this present life. More and more the role of the Church will be seen as preaching the salvific message of Christ and being mediation and witness to Christ's grace. The activity of the Church will lean more on the side of the strictly spiritual and religious, of being the sacrament of salvation for all men, of giving a testimony of poverty, renunciation, eschatological hope and disinterested charity. The Church will have its influence and its impact in the fullness of the Christian paradox, in being insignificant as an earthly organization and yet all important in the order of salvation, attracting all men without any human attractiveness, strong in her weakness and because of her weakness, at the same time a stumbling block and ark of salvation.

I have presented some elements of what currently would be described, I suppose, as a dialogue between the Church and contemporary civilization. A dialogue entails exchange of words and ideas, entails listening to what the other has to say, entails a certain amount of understanding and sympathy. I have attempted to describe a dialogue that entails something more: an exchange of realities, of values, a true and mutually beneficial interchange. This is part of that internal vital process in the Church that we call adaptation. This adaptation is not a desire to be accepted by the world; it has nothing to do with the machinations of the social climber or the tactics of the parvenu who craves for a little place in a society that ignores him and in which he does not really belong. Adaptation in the Church's case is the desire of being present, of being there, in the midst of men, intelligible, available, open: a sign of salvation for all men mysteriously shrouded in human, all too human, appearances and yet efficacious as the presence of the eschatologically victorious grace of Christ. But the Church is not forgetful that together with this pressing urge of her internal being to adapt in order to remain faithful to herself, she carries Christ's heritage of rejection, of not being accepted. The Church will maintain always while in this world the nature of a stranger in a foreign land, preaching a scandalous wisdom, pressing forward amid persecutions and consolations, "announcing the cross and death of the Lord until he comes" (1 Cor 11:26) and revealing to the world, faithfully though darkly, the mystery of its Lord, until in the end, it will be manifested in full light.

~~~~~~

The Death of God
in Recent Protestant Theology

DAVID J. STAGAMAN, S.J.

My Protestant has no God, has no faith in God, and affirms
both the death of God and the death of all the forms of
theism. Even so, he is not primarily a man of negation,
for if there is a movement away from God and religion,
there is the more important movement into, for, towards the
world, worldly life, and the neighbor as the bearer of the
worldly Jesus.[1]

The preceding words were excerpted from an article by William
Hamilton entitled "The Death of God Theologies Today."
They are his description of a current movement within Protes-
tant theology which is the topic of the present essay. The goal
of the essay is that the reader will come to understand what
Hamilton means by the words just quoted.

At the outset two observations are in order. First, in any discussion of the death-of-God theologians, each participant should
keep in mind that he is not concerned with a large group of
Protestant theologians. Their number is small, though apparently
increasing; and their influence is not yet widespread. They
acquired notoriety after an article in the religion section of
Time magazine,[2] followed by numerous articles in the popular

---

[1] William Hamilton, "The Death of God Theologies Today," in *Radical
Theology and The Death of God Theology* by Thomas J. J. Altizer and
William Hamilton (Indianapolis: Bobbs-Merrill, 1966), p. 37.

[2] "Christian Atheism: The God is Dead Movement," *Time,* October 22,
1965, pp. 61–62.

press. Thus far the attention they have received from the public
has exceeded their impact upon professional Protestant theology.

A second observation is that the reader might well appreciate
a few remarks on bibliography. A succinct presentation from a
moderate viewpoint of the concerns which preoccupy the thinking of the death-of-God theologians can be found in John
Robinson's *The New Reformation*.[3] *The Death of God* by
Gabriel Vahanian is a more thorough treatment from the same
point of view which traces the sources of God's demise in the
post-Christian world.[4]

The work of the radical theologians (as they prefer to be
called) can best be sampled from three of their books: *Radical
Theology and The Death of God Theology*, a compilation of
the best articles written by Thomas J. J. Altizer and William
Hamilton before May of 1966;[5] Altizer's *The Gospel of Christian
Atheism*;[6] and Hamilton's more readable *The New Essence of
Christianity*.[7] *The Secular Meaning of the Gospel*[8] by Paul Van
Buren, who in spite of his protests is ordinarily included among
the death-of-God theologians, is best mentioned in the context
of radical theology.

A number of good critical analyses of death-of-God theology
are now available. For a sprightly, brief, yet accurate criticism,
Kenneth Hamilton's *God is Dead: The Anatomy of a Slogan*[9] is
recommended. Thomas Ogletree in *The Death of God Controversy*,[10] which is at once scholarly and readable, explains and

---

[3] John Robinson, *The New Reformation* (Philadelphia: Westminster
Press, 1965).

[4] Gabriel Vahanian, *The Death of God: The Culture of our Post-
Christian Era* (New York: George Braziller, 1961).

[5] See footnote 1.

[6] Thomas J. J. Altizer, *The Gospel of Christian Atheism* (Philadelphia:
Westminster Press, 1966).

[7] William Hamilton, *The New Essence of Christianity*, Revised edition
(New York: Association Press, 1966).

[8] Paul Van Buren, *The Secular Meaning of the Gospel* (New York:
Macmillin, 1965).

[9] Kenneth Hamilton, *God is Dead: The Anatomy of a Slogan* (Grand
Rapids: William B. Eerdmans, 1966).

[10] Thomas Ogletree, *The Death of God Controversy* (Nashville: Abing-
don Press, 1966).

evaluates the writings of Altizer, Hamilton, and Van Buren. The work of Robinson and Van Buren is profoundly discussed by Mascall in *The Secularization of Christianity*.[11]

In the course of this essay, the reader will hopefully become aware that the term, death-of-God theologian, covers a diverse grouping of Protestant thinkers; it includes both moderates and radicals. If the author's endeavor is successful, the reader will also have become acquainted with the death-of-God theology of three specific men: first, Bishop John Robinson, the author of *Honest to God*, as a spokesman for the moderates; then as spokesmen for the radicals, Thomas J. J. Altizer of Emory University and William Hamilton of Colgate Rochester Divinity School.

The distinction between moderate and radical in death-of-God theology turns principally about two issues: what God is dead, and what function does the Church have in the contemporary world? For a moderate, the God who is dead is the God of religiosity, the God whom men have created in their own image to have their will done; the Church finds itself in an era when experimentation is imperative if the God of the Bible is to be conveyed to the man of today. For a radical, the God who is dead is the transcendent God of traditional Christianity; and the Church where the Word is preached and the sacraments administered is no longer a viable instrument for the salvation of men.

In an appendix to his book, *The New Reformation*,[12] Bishop John Robinson asks himself: Can a truly contemporary person not be an atheist? There seem to be three reasons why he should be: God is intellectually superfluous; He is emotionally dispensable; He is morally intolerable.

God is intellectually superfluous. Laplace said all there was to be said in answer to Napoleon's question about the place of God in his astronomical system: "I have no need of that hypothesis." The contemporary scientist knows that his freedom of inquiry dates from the liberation of his science from the bondage

[11] E. L. Mascall, *The Secularization of Christianity* (New York: Holt, Rinehart, and Winston, 1965).
[12] Robinson, *op. cit.*, pp. 106–122.

of Christian theology. The God who is the ultimate explanation of all things is the God who for centuries retarded the growth of modern science and would not permit men to find satisfaction in an empirical explanation of phenomena.

God is also emotionally dispensable. Contemporary man no longer asks the Good Lord to provide. He realizes, with Marx, that the provident God, in whom his grandmother believed, was a projection of human inadequacies into a future life where God would see that all was restored. Modern man no longer needs this God; he believes in himself and other men. For instance, when modern man boards an airplane, he puts his trust in the pilot and not in God.

Finally, God is morally intolerable. This is the God who causes human suffering and tragedy; and, furthermore, He requires us to accept these things as His will for us. Contemporary man dislikes this God most of all for he sees Him as the arch-foe of all human progress. He is the God who forces us to accept the suffering and death by disease as a manifestation of a higher will instead of being driven to search out the natural causes of the disease.

Bishop Robinson faces the aforementioned difficulties of contemporary man with the traditional God by means of an I-Thou analysis of Christian belief. There are three possible types of relationships with other persons. The first is a functional relationship in which we make use of the other; our faith in God must never be an attempt to use God. Second, our relationship with the other can be one of cooperative union. Our faith must never be this: equal partnership with God. Faith must be the third type of relationship which alone is personal; that is, a relationship in which we love and trust God for His own sake. For the Christian, this love and trust will be explicitly directed toward Christ and His Father. But, according to Bishop Robinson, faith need not be so explicit. An atheist who devotedly serves some absolute ideal might well be carrying on a personal I-Thou relationship with God.

In either case, for the man who loves and trusts God for His own sake, God remains intellectually superfluous. He is never to be inserted into a system as an ultimate explanation; He remains exclusively a subject of encounter.

God continues to be emotionally dispensable. For the man of God realizes that providence means that God's saving activity is present in every event, not that there is a special divine causality looking out for what man thinks best. Thus, when a Christian boards an airplane, he trusts in God to save him and in the pilot to get the plane off the ground.

Finally, God is still morally intolerable. He is not an absentee controller who permits suffering, but the crucified figure who transfigures human suffering. His aim is not to retard the human quest after medical cures, but to enable us to bear the inevitable suffering that comes our way.

For Thomas J. J. Altizer, modern theology began with Kierkegaard and Nietzsche.[13] For Kierkegaard, authentic human existence was existence in faith. God had died in the sense that He was no longer to be known as an objective reality. Faith, as a consequence, became a leap out of history, liberating man from existence in the realm of objectivity to an inward communion with God within the depths of his being. Nietzsche realized, as have Heidegger and Sartre since, that man is a being wholly caught up in time; thus the ground for subjective faith by a leap out of history was dissolved. Nietzsche further realized that authentic existence in the modern world was possible for the believer and unbeliever alike; hence the death of God had permeated even to man's subjective life. Kierkegaard did away with the possibility of God being an objective reality; Nietzsche did away with the possibility of God being a subject of encounter. What then is left for the Christian theologian? Only to affirm the death of the God of Christianity and to embrace an existence which is wholly contained within the world. For Altizer, however, Nietzsche's insight did not emerge outside an historical context; it came as an expected outcome to the history of Christian theological thought.

According to Altizer, the Christian theological tradition has

---

[13] Altizer, *Radical Theology and The Death of God*, pp. 95–111.

been untrue to Jesus and the Kingdom of God He proclaimed.[14]
This Kingdom had three essential characteristics: it expected an
immediate end of the world by transformation, reversal, or
dissolution; it subordinated mythical visions of the end to a
moral obedience in response to the end; finally, it called its
followers out of history to a new reality — faith.

All three characteristics of the Kingdom of God proclaimed
by Jesus have been abandoned during the development of Christian thought. First, the Kingdom has a world-denying thrust;
it says that the world is only temporary, soon to come to an
end. But Christian theologians, after they came into contact
with Greek philosophical thought, became obsessed with the
notion of being and thereby became world-affirming. The categories of ontology were utilized to describe both God and
man. Again, the Kingdom, as an ethical imperative, summons
man to deny himself. But Christian thought has centered on man
as autonomous and focused its attention on what man had to
do in this world in order to be saved in the next. Finally, the
Kingdom calls men out of history to believe in the God of the
End, who is bringing history to an end. Bultmann keenly
appreciated this anti-historical aspect of the Kingdom when he
described its founder as a faith-event, and thus removed Jesus
from the arena of scientific investigation. What most Christian
theologians have done, however, has been to search out patterns
and directions in history which prove that the hand of the
transcendent God touches human events. They have failed to
appreciate that the Kingdom of God is antithetical to such
thinking. Thus the contemporary theologian must realize that
he is faced with a horrifying choice: either the Kingdom of
God or the Christian theological tradition.

Therefore, in order to understand accurately the Kingdom
proclaimed by Jesus, Altizer believes that he must look not to
his Christian past but elsewhere. The approach he selects is a
comparison of New Testament eschatological faith with the

---

[14] Altizer, "The Religious Meaning of Myth and Symbol," in *Truth,
Myth, and Symbol*, eds. Thomas Altizer, William Beardslee, and J. Harvey
Young (Englewood Cliffs: Prentice-Hall, 1962), pp. 87–108.

quest of oriental mystics for Nirvana.[15] Altizer discovers that the oriental mystics do not seek the divine in the familiar modes of conscious life, but that they seek an experience in which all consciousness of external reality and the self is lost. Within this realm of pure experience, the oriental mystic discovers a primordial beginning, a paradise prior to the sin which now infects the consciousness of both the self and the world. Oriental mysticism is, then, essentially a backward-moving process which traverses the sinful past by blotting out its consciousness until the mystic arrives at Nirvana, the paradise of man's original innocence.

Oriental mysticism has a feature in common with the Kingdom of God preached by Jesus. Buddha forbade all theoretical questions because he grasped that all abstract thought is antithetical to true religious experience. Likewise, maintains Altizer,[16] the eschatological preaching of the prophets, among whom Jesus is the greatest, never produced a theology. Only Judaism and Christianity produced theologies, and neither school of thought has been true to its sources.

By contrast, oriental mysticism also directs attention to the true nature of Jesus' eschatological preaching. He preached a message which was essentially oriented to the future. He summoned His followers to deny the world, that is, the past, and called them to faith, that is, to believe in the future. For Jesus stands at the summit of the prophetic tradition and the prophets' subjection of the faith of their fathers to rational scrutiny.[17] In ancient Israel, men had lived by myth and ritual. They composed myths about their forefathers and the traditional shrines. Certain ritualistic acts of worship were devised to commemorate the great deeds of the ancestors and the important incidents at the shrines. The purpose of such mythology and ritual was to enable the ancient Israelite to achieve a harmony between himself, the world, and the hallowed or sacred. In this

[15] Altizer, "Nirvana and the Kingdom of God," in *New Theology*, No. 1, eds. Martin Marty and Dean Peerman (New York: Macmillan, 1964), pp. 150–168; and *The Gospel of Christian Atheism*, pp. 31–40.
[16] Altizer, "Nirvana and the Kingdom of God."
[17] Altizer, "Religious Meaning of Myth and Symbol."

era the notion of transcendence was born as an axiological center around which all the myths and rituals were organized.

But the religion of the ancients could not bear rational scrutiny. In the face of emergent rational consciousness, the religion of early Israel led to a reversal of itself; this reversal took the form of the prophetic-eschatological tradition. In this second stage of Israel's religious development, the emphasis shifted from myths and rituals which were communal acts to the faith of the individual believers. The old values became interiorized, and the ancient ideal of harmony was recast in terms of a God of judgment who would restore all in all.

What Jesus accomplished was the complete reversal of Israel's religious thinking. The ancient Israelites through myth and ritual had attempted to transform the profane into the sacred by changing concrete times and places into sacred times and places. The prophets, when they summoned Israel to interiorize its religion (as Kierkegaard has done in modern Protestantism), tried to make the sacred and the profane antithetical categories. What Jesus did was to reunite the sacred and the profane by transforming the sacred into the profane through His doctrine of the Incarnation.

Jesus proclaimed in the Incarnation that the transcendent God, in whom the fathers of Israel believed, had become incarnate in Him, Jesus. God had thus become flesh; that is, He had shed His transcendence in order to become wholly contained in our history. In the Incarnation, therefore, the transcendent God of the Judaeo-Christian tradition died. He no longer exists because He took on and became immersed in the human condition.[18]

Thus, the dilemma of the contemporary Christian theologian has been solved. He no longer has to accept the mythological view of early Israel and Christian theology along with their transcendent God. Nor does he have to accept the world-denying mentality of the prophetic and Kierkegaardian traditions which irrevocably separate man from the world he would otherwise love. With Nietzsche, as Altizer interprets him, the contempo-

---

[18] Altizer, *The Gospel of Christian Atheism,* pp. 40–75.

rary theologian realizes that in the Incarnation the transcendent God has died as a real event of history, and that the summons to faith in Jesus is a call to radical immanence.

Today's Christian is asked to make an act of dialectical faith: he must deny the realm of transcendence in order to affirm the wholly immanent reality of modern man; he turns from the domain of the sacred to that of the radically profane which alone can be the sanctuary for today's sacred. And, paradoxically, when he does so, the Christian begins to appropriate for himself the meaning of the Incarnation. For he begins to grasp that a truly contemporary Word must be detached from the Jesus of history and become incarnate in our flesh. Thus the Incarnation requires that we become truly contemporary; and this demands that we embrace the full reality of our history in which the death of God is a real event and await the epiphany of a new word of faith.

William Hamilton has made the following observation about the work of Altizer:

> Altizer's vision is an exciting one, logically imprecise, calculated to make empiricists weep, but imaginatively and religiously it is both sophisticated and powerful.[19]

These words are high compliment because William Hamilton alone in this country shares prominence with Altizer as a radical theologian.

Hamilton describes himself as an alienated man. He is first alienated from any sort of God who comes as a fulfiller of needs or a solver of problems. He has rejected this God on three counts. The first is the failure of modern theologians to locate any religious *a priori*, a part of self or a part of human experience that needs God.[20] God today, he thinks, has been reduced to one of the possible alternatives in the radically pluralistic intellectual and spiritual milieu of contemporary man. The second reason for rejecting the traditional God is that man today has come of age.[21] He trusts the world to fulfill his needs and

---

[19] Hamilton, "The Death of God Theologies Today," p. 31.
[20] *Ibid.*, pp. 37–41.
[21] *Ibid.*

solve his problems. If God is to have meaning to man come of age, then He must assume another role. The final reason is that the impotence of God has been revealed by the problem of evil.[22] What, Hamilton asks, can Christians say in explanation of why a child has died? The assertion that God has done so for such and such a reason no longer rings true. For men today know that the inevitability of suffering and death overtook even God's son. The only God acceptable to contemporary men is a God who is impotent to overcome evil but has become one with them in submitting to suffering and death.

Hamilton also finds himself alienated from the Church.[23] The Church, he says, can have three meanings. First, it can be one, holy, catholic, and apostolic; this notion he finds useful in ecumenical dialogue. Secondly, the Church is found wherever the Word of God is preached and the sacraments rightly administered; this notion he finds congenial in his vocation as a teacher of theology. But only the final notion does Hamilton find religiously meaningful. This is the Church that is found whenever Christ is being formed among men in the world.

As a consequence, Hamilton has moved to his present theological stance. This stance has a negative aspect; for he finds himself reduced to asserting that God and the traditional forms of theism are dead. Hamilton describes himself as a passive man, waiting in silence and praying for his losses to be returned. While he waits, he searches for a language and a style by which Christians can once again stand before God and delight in His presence as Augustine once did.[24]

Yet Hamilton's theology is not all negativity. It has a positive aspect of discipleship to Jesus. He defines the Christian as a man bound to Jesus, obedient to Him as He was obedient. Yet this Christian is a man who has lost faith and hope. For him, Jesus is not an object or ground of faith, not a person, event, or community, but a place to be. The Christian without faith and hope does have love and the example of Jesus Christ;

---

[22] Hamilton, *The New Essence of Christianity*, pp. 44–55.
[23] Hamilton, *Radical Theology and The Death of God*, p. 91.
[24] *Ibid.*, pp. 41 and 92.

he does not know what he is looking for, but he does know where to be — at his neighbor's side.[25]

For Hamilton, the death of God is a metaphor. It describes the predicament of the contemporary theologian. In one essay[26] Hamilton describes the theologian of today as a man who has turned from Oedipus to Orestes, and from Hamlet to Prospero. He has left behind the inner anguish of an Oedipus or a Hamlet. Like Orestes, he has freely killed his mother in affirming the death of God; like Prospero, he has abjured his magic by rejecting all traditional theism. And like both Orestes and Prospero, he has done so in order to assume his princely duties in the world.

In a sense, the task assigned at the beginning of this essay is now completed. The reader is now somewhat acquainted with the work of Bishop John Robinson, Thomas Altizer, and William Hamilton. Hopefully, he also sees that between the moderates and the radicals, there is a difference about which God is to be killed and what Church is to be done away with.

In conclusion, it does seem appropriate that a few comments be made about the theological method of Hamilton and Altizer, since their radical theology has had such an impact upon the American theological scene. The flaw in methodology can be roughly characterized as a certain unwillingness to live with mystery. This unwillingness is most apparent in their critiques of the solutions of Barth, Bultmann, and Tillich as half-measures. For Altizer and Hamilton all the solutions of the great neo-orthodox Protestants are inadequate because the divine transcendence and immanence are never entirely reconciled. That Barth, Bultmann, and Tillich realized that divine attributes are mysteries surpassing human understanding, and that all theological endeavor must eventually terminate in incomplete expressions, never appears in the critiques of the radical theologians.

Altizer and Hamilton insist that theological evidence must be of the same nature as that of any other type of human inquiry. The former analyzes the history of Israel and the Church and

---

[25] *Ibid.*, pp. 40–42 and 46–50.
[26] *Ibid.*, pp. 42–45.

then compares Christianity with non-Christian religions until he
has sufficient data with which he can frame a coherent explanation. The latter searches the domains of literature and of his
personal experience so that he might formulate an explanation
of authentic religious existence.

Both Altizer and Hamilton insist on theologizing alone. They
have irrevocably separated themselves from their theological
traditions, both pre- and post-Reformation, since all past explanations have proved inadequate for the discerning theological
eye. They prefer explanations which are totally within human
grasp; hence their unbelief.

The Christian believer, however, begins in the realization that
faith is a type of human knowing different from scientific
inquiry. He appreciates that he believes in a God who is a
mystery, and that any inquiry into the divine will yield at best
partial solutions. He simultaneously affirms that God is transcendent, that is, beyond history and all human inquiry, and
that God has become immanent in our history through His
revelation and therefore is partially accessible to human knowing.

Christian theology is thinking in this faith. The Christian
theologian constantly attempts to explain why and what he
believes; but he realizes that the only sufficient explanation is
God, and consequently the answer will be inextricably en-
shrouded in mystery. Thus, the inadequacy of all past theological expressions comes as no scandal; all such explanations,
even his own, are condemned to be somewhat insufficient. He
is thus led not to reject his past, but to accept the challenge
of improving upon it.

As the Christian theologian pursues an improved understanding of God's seemingly irreconcilable transcendence and immanence, he has one consolation. He knows that he does so
not alone, but as a member of a people, God's people, all of
whom are committed to understanding better the God in whom
they believe and who ever eludes containment in their best
expressions of what He is.

There is something intriguing, however, about the final stance
that both Altizer and Hamilton assume: they are completely

taken up with service to the profane or to the neighbor, confident that within their commitment will emerge a new ground for faith. And here lies the core of the problem for all death-of-God theologians: how can a man be both contemporary and Christian? How can the Christian assume his secular responsibilities?

And it is here that I find them most Christian: first, in their concern to be contemporary; and, second, in their conviction that the Christian can and must be so. And even if I should disagree over their methodology and feel that they have cut the ground of Christian contemporaneousness out from under themselves by abandoning the Christian tradition, the death-of-God theologians do serve to remind me of a significant truth: that God does die in the world He created and redeemed whenever His people are found incapable of demonstrating their contemporaneousness.

Whenever God Dies: Protestant Roots of the Problem of God

MARTIN E. MARTY

Lately, whenever God dies, it seems as if a Protestant stands by as witness. Whenever God is killed, the knife of a Protestant is left behind as a clue, as evidence. Is the secret out at last, after four and a half centuries, that the final logic of Protestantism is atheism?

People who use the language about "the death of God" in the Western Christian tradition regularly point out the differences between their vision and that of classic atheism. Classic atheism is timeless. It is a purely philosophical commitment, made independently of human events. It asserts that God is not, that God never was. Whoever has been rooted in the Christian tradition of the West finds such language difficult. If he uses his terms carefully, he finds that as he moves out of the community in which a language of faith has been appropriate, classic atheism is found to be inappropriate. God, for him and in his circle of language, was alive and has been killed. He speaks of "the death of God" as an event.

"Death of God" in Protestant Symbolism

Seen in such a light, the language of the "death of God" is mythical or metaphorical. Whoever employs it is dealing phenomenologically with the human venture. He is exploring the experience of consciousness and reporting his research and observation. Whoever uses the phenomenological approach does not claim, when he witnesses to the "death of God," that he has had a voyage to a transcendent realm of experience. He cannot demonstrate the presence of the corpse: If his prophecies suggest that he can, careful examination will reveal that he *is* talking metaphorically or symbolically. Just as when once he spoke on the context of faith he had to resort to symbolic language, even when he referred to God as Father or Lord, so now if he speaks of the "death of God" after he has once implied a living God, he refers symbolically to events in human culture or in individual and personal experience.

If it is true that the witness to the "death of God" deals phenomenologically with experience, then we may fruitfully observe the witness, the one who claims the experience. In the forms in which "death of God" talk impinges on our particular culture, the speakers are often of Protestant lineage, and thus it is possible to trace a number of Protestant theological roots for such talk and experience.

The attempt to see a Protestant background to the experience "whenever God dies" is not made in a provincial institutional sense. The witness or prophet need not by any means be or have been a member of a church called Protestant. Needless to say, the "death of God" vision is not part of the orthodox substance of Protestantism! Nor should one claim that no versions of "death of God" experience have ever occurred or are not occurring on terrain where Roman Catholicism has been basic. Whoever has seen a Fellini film, read a page of Sartre, observed either casual disregard for or enraged opposition to the living God in Italy, Spain, or Latin America, would not allow Protestantism in the institutional sense the privilege or responsibility of staking out a monopolistic claim. God has died in sundry times and diverse manners.

Apparently there are tendencies or predispositions which, if carried to logical extreme or handled undialectically, expose Protestants to "death of God" talk. One can slightly invert or pervert basic Protestant teachings and in the process be set out on the "death of God" course. No doubt theological and non-theological factors alike have to be introduced on this

course. We could begin on a waggish note, for example, and
suggest that Protestants have had these predispositions because
they have parsonages, and Roman Catholics do not. The teacher
of church history, as he deals with nineteenth-century "god-
killers" in Germany or Great Britain, notes with wearying
frequency as a first line in the biography of his subject, that
he was "born in a parsonage." Evidently the parsonage, which
has produced so many natural-born witnesses to the living God,
also spawns many who have reacted and, out of their Projects
Head-Start, have developed impulses to witness the "death
of God."

Such a note may provide an important psychological clue to
our subject, but we leave to those trained in psychology the
task of tracking it down. Here it would be a frivolous and
side-tracking venture. We are asking: What tendencies integral
to Protestant witness predispose people toward the experience
of the "death of God"? The list cannot be comprehensive; it
is at best suggestive. Since Protestantism is so filled with
variety, we shall often have occasion to note particularist strands
in its tradition, not letting the part speak for the whole. Inevitably, we shall find ourselves concentrating chiefly on those
Protestant moments to which contemporary users of "death of
God" language have their appeal.

The Lutherans Sang "God Is Dead"

Most commentators trace the origin of the modern use of
the phrase to Hegel, who himself was adapting a line from a
Lutheran chorale by Johann Rist. There we hear that on Good
Friday "Gott selbst ist tot."[1]

> O sorrow dread,
> Our God is dead.

It is from this Lutheran experience of identification with the
disciples of the death of Jesus that one kind of "death of God"
language grew.

While early Calvinism was more concerned with a tran-

---

[1] Recent Lutheran hymnals in America have softened the shock
of this hymn by translating it, "God's Son is dead."

scendent God made manifest, Lutheranism spoke of an immanent God who remained hidden in history but who was
revealed as nowhere else in Jesus Christ. This occurred su-
premely in His self-giving and loving death on the cross. For
Hegel, the resurrection was the historian's anticlimax to this
death; the death alone had had something to do with religion.[2]

The hymn in question was, of course, not a full statement of
evangelical faith concerning the meaning of the event of the
cross. In fuller dogmatic exposition the Lutherans took time
to make clear that when they said "Jesus is dead," while this
related to the affirmation that in Jesus dwelt bodily all the fullness of the Godhead, they did not mean to exhaust all that
believers had to say in witness to God. The phrase was devo-
tional, poetic, unguarded — and it was all that Hegel needed
to exploit a viewpoint which he personally wanted to see
enlarged. Now the "kenosis" or the self-emptying of God in
Jesus (Philippians, Chapter Two) was employed to obscure
any distinctions between divine and human natures in Jesus.
Now a man was able, according to Hegel, to participate in the
"Golgotha of absolute spirit" and to do without false religious
props entirely as he underwent spiritual crisis.

Hegel moved on from this point to engage in polemic against
the Reformation's stress on resurrection from death as violating
the meaning of the "Golgotha of absolute spirit" and against
the Enlightenment for resorting to a Deism in which God
has always been a philosophical abstraction and not a living
presence. It is possible at this point to leave the Hegelian trail,
having visited it chiefly to pick up the Lutheran hymn whose
phrase spoke so eloquently to him. Nietzsche was later to make
more of the Hegelian experience, and contemporary "death of
God" spokesmen enlarge upon Nietzsche's proclamation. We
can here replace the familiar "In the Beginning was Hegel"[3]
with a less familiar and almost startling phrase: "In the Beginning

---

[2] Hegel, *The Phenomenology of Mind* (London, 1961), pp. 753, 808;
Modern Library version (New York: Random House, 1953), p. 506.

[3] A chapter heading in Étienne Borne, *Atheism* (New York: Hawthorn,
1961), p. 35.

was a Lutheran chorale." Hegel, Nietzche, and our contemporaries witness the "death of God" out of a surprising variety of motives and interests, but they are united in one concern: to use it as the fundamental experience for regarding death and their death and thus of life and their life.

Earlier "God-killing" Agencies

Accidental and unsustained witness to the "death of God" was older than Rist's chorale, of course. The mystics had hinted at it in some of the language of the *via negativa*. It is possible to see god-killing tendencies in the biblical moves toward the desacralization of nature and the secularization of politics. In the record of these moves, of course, ultimate witness to the living God is undoubted and clear; the processes of exorcism and iconoclasm had already been set in motion. Later some readers saw in these prophetic processes the resultant establishment of nature and history as autonomies, divorced from their original rootages in Being or in God's Person. Through another misreading, the Bible's injunctions against idolatry and its prophetic criticism of religion could be carried to the point of witness to the "death of God" Himself.

Catholic orthodoxy in the era of the creeds (as at Chalcedon in 451) or in the high medieval scholasticism worked to uphold the view which saw nature and history rooted in the activity of a living God and grounded in a context in which the Lordship of Jesus Christ was recognized. At the same time, Chalcedon worked to set the divine and human natures of Jesus into complementarity in such a way that language like Rist's should have been forestalled. Between the scholastic synthesis and post-Reformation piety something had occurred which made possible an obscuring of clear witness to a Living God after His kenosis and death in Jesus on the cross.

"Death of God" language is never directly logically appropriate in the Reformation tradition. It results from neglect of some evangelical resources and the emphatic assertion of others (as in Hegel: on Good Friday at the expense of Easter). This must be kept in mind as we survey a number of Protestant contributions to "death of God" language.

The Theology of the Cross and the Problem of God

At the heart of the problem lies an accent in Luther's epistemology. Here, it must be noted, Calvinism took a different course and in some ways, at least temporarily, exempted itself from Lutheran problems with God-language. It would not be unfair to say that historically the problem of God has been more acute on Lutheran soil than on Reformed soil, where theocratic tendencies in politics established a pattern for general witness to an accessible God. Not until the accessibility of this sovereign God was distorted, until He became, in Perry Miller's terms, a "chained God,"[4] and thus, not until the language of complete immanence created a cultural degrading of the reality of God, is it unsurprising to encounter "death of God" language in the Reformed tradition or in the heresies it has spawned.

Luther, in order to clear his accent on God's grace in the justification of man, railed against any attempts to see any aspect of man's personhood or equipment capable of being employed to gain merit or from the purposes of making a claim on God. Nowhere was his polemic more violent than it was against the Schoolmen's practice of attempting to speak with confidence concerning the hidden God (as Luther referred to Him). Such speaking was "speculative philosophy" which betrayed man into spiritual pride and blindness; he no longer recognized his need for Christ's sacrifice. Thus in this context (but in this context only[5]) reason became the "Devil's damned whore" and stood in the way of man's acceptance of grace. Man's whole old Adam, old self, had to be annihilated by the Law and Wrath of God before the new creation was enacted and the new, forgiven man was brought forth. In this activity and enactment God was manifest even though He remained partly veiled; He looks, indeed, like a loving but virtually powerless God in the death of Jesus Christ.

How is God to be known, then, since speculative reason and a doctrine of God based on constructive philosophy were to be

[4] See Chapter III, "The Marrow of Puritan Divinity" in Perry Miller, *Errand into the Wilderness* (Cambridge: Harvard University Press, 1956).

[5] See B. A. Gerrish, *Grace and Reason: A Study in the Theology of Luther* (Oxford: Clarendon Press, 1964).

ruled out? Luther seldom wavered from the clarity with which he described his approach to the knowledge of God in the Heidelberg Disputation of 1518:[6]

> 18. It is certain that a man must completely despair of himself in order to become fit to obtain the grace of Christ.
> 19. The one who beholds what is invisible of God, through the perception of what is made (cf. Romans 1:20), is not rightly called a theologian.
> 20. But rather the one who perceives what is visible of God, God's "backside" (Exodus 33:23), by beholding the sufferings and the cross.
> 21. The "theologian of glory" calls the bad good and the good bad. The "theologian of the cross" says what a thing is.

Ever after, the philosophical roots of theism were called into question in some portions of Protestantism. So long as evangelicals in the Lutheran tradition lived in a world in which the narrative of the revelation of God in Christ's cross was itself not suspect, the acute problem of "doing without philosophy" in the constructive task itself was not evident. It was to become so by the nineteenth century when the crisis of historical relativism was heightened in Germany.

Today's "death of God" theologians recapture the Protestant and particularly the Lutheran delight in the theology of the cross, the visible things of God, in the empirical and the phenomenological. They profess to have little difficulty in recognizing their involvement in His Golgotha. Some of them are even prepared to say that in Jesus, God was alive and then, in the death of Jesus, God died. As Hegel did before them, they suppress the Reformation's sustained witness to the power of the resurrection either because it seems to remove them from the boundaries of the empirical or because it seems to deprive men of the valid expression of the "death of God" through an anticlimactic experience like resurrection, an event which would rob death of its drama or effectuality.

If it is true that in the 1960's American Protestantism is witnessing the break-up of formulations derived from men like

---

[6] In John Dillenberger (ed.), *Martin Luther* (New York: Doubleday Anchor, 1961), p. 502 f.

Karl Barth and Paul Tillich, one should be able to recognize here an accent in Barth. Dietrich Bonhoeffer once spoke, somewhat unfairly, of Barth's theology as a "positivism of revelation."[7] "Eat, bird, or die!" Barth seemed to be saying to Bonhoeffer's generation as he spoke of revelation in what appeared to be levelled but demanding terms. But later it was the meaning of revelation itself that was being called into question; it was the occasion of revelation itself that was being doubted. This meaning and this occasion were to become central in a new generation's theological quest. In too many ways Barth had disallowed such inquiries. They would have reopened philosophical questions which he had to rule out as inappropriate, insoluble, and obstructive of God's justifying activity in Christ.

The problem of God behind an epistemology which relied exclusively on "grammar applied to the Scripture," on history and exegesis, was not live to Luther any more than it was to his Catholic contemporaries. When John Osborne in his play *Luther* causes Luther to doubt the existence of God or to agonize over His reality (in short, to puzzle over the "death of God"), Luther experts speak critically of the play. Luther's doubts dealt with the life of grace in God's bearing toward man and not with the life of God Himself. Luther knew of *Anfechtungen*, spiritual doubts and temptations permitted and even caused by God. But these came because his awareness of a living and wrathful God was too vivid, not because it had become so pale.

After Kant, after access to the noumenal is itself called into question, Protestants who leaned toward Luther's epistemology found new occasion to heighten their distrust of speculative philosophy as a mode of discussing the reality of God. The erosive modern experience robbed them of many features which Luther could still take for granted. The theology of the cross, described as a protection for man's frail faith and an assurance of the love of God, could by a twist of fate and through the torture of history work against faith, assurance, or recogni-

[7] Dietrich Bonhoeffer, *Prisoner for God* (New York: Macmillan, 1957), p. 126.

tion of the life of God. It was all well and good to deal with the "visibles" of God, but how did one make the jump from "beholding the sufferings and the cross" to any objective reality called "God"? With this question, we are not far from the normative experience of many modern "death of God" thinkers.

Transcendent Immanence and Immanent Transcendence

Lest it seem as if Lutheranism bears all the burden in this issue, let it be noted that while Bonhoeffer is of Lutheran lineage, Barth stands in the Reformed tradition. How is it appropriate to introduce his name in this context? For one thing, Barth has been strongly influenced by Luther in many matters; for another, the Kantian stress which complicates metaphysical thought in relation to God is strong in Barth. Most of all — and now it is time to involve Reformed Protestantism directly and frontally — from Calvin and Zwingli on, the Reformed tradition in Protestantism has also seen difficulties in witness to God behind the "sufferings and the cross" of Jesus Christ.

Calvin spiritualized and individualized the sense of the presence of God. Luther said, in effect, that God was "not the God of the philosophers" (to jump a century and more to borrow from Pascal); he was not evident in sacerdotal society, in the orders of Christendom. He was hidden in them and in the weak and powerless things of the world, including death. For Calvin, God also was not evident in hierarchical orders but was manifest in the individual's spiritual life as the Sovereign whose election of his own is experienced, and through which experience he is known. Calvin seems to "pull rank" at the foot of the cross, however, and to exempt the elect from the experience of the "death of God." To translate this symbolic episode in the life of spiritual man into the theological or philosophical mode: here was the open window for a trace of "theology of glory." But Calvin (and after him Barth), who had spoken so radically on God's otherness, His inscrutibility, His majesty, is in the end ready to make Him accessible, as it were, in new hierarchies and orders — this time in the experience of the faithful and the elect. Here God becomes manifest. In the

Lutheran approach there is danger that God and man become identified and "God" be swallowed. Erich Przywara put it provocatively:

> Thus the Lutheran "lumping" of grace and faith is exaggerated into an "identification." "God's thought in us" is "God's being in us," immanence carried to identity.

Przywara saw this Lutheran note (we die — Christ dies — God dies) being overcome from within by Søren Kierkegaard, and being carried on in modern Protestantism as a programme by Karl Barth, who wanted to "overcome Lutheran immanentism by an uncompromising doctrine of God's transcendence." But Przywara saw in Calvin and Kierkegaard and Barth "transcendence even to paradox" as another formal principle which interpenetrated with the Lutheran version of epistemology and experience. For the Hegelian-Lutheran line "immanence is carried to such an extent that man is God" and thus "absorption of God" issues in atheism.

> Kierkegaard's paradox involves the consequence that thought when its object is God is doomed of its very nature to encounter in solitude the "Unknown." If in Hegel an "Absorption of God" issues in atheism, the logic of Kierkegaard's paradox, when unswervingly carried through, atheism proceeds from "despair of God."

Przywara, it must be noted, eventually rescued Hegel and Kierkegaard by the use of Augustinian motifs and saw in both an eventual or at least a potential Catholicization in the interests of the grace of a living God. But before he did this, interrupting the logic of their positions at the crucial mid-point, he succeded in showing that Lutheranism and Calvinism represented "six of one and a half dozen of the other" in the Lutheran contradiction of "transcendent immanence" and the Calvinist contradiction of "immanent transcendence."[8] When Karl Barth late in his career was to write a book called, in English, *The Humanity of God*[9] he came close to identifying with the Lutheran version of the contradiction or paradox.

---

[8] Erich Przywara, S.J., in *Saint Augustine* (by M. C. D'Arcy, S.J., and others) (New York: Meridian, 1957), p. 268 ff.

[9] See the book of that title, published by John Knox of Richmond, 1960.

Nothing that I have said here is to suggest that "the living God" is dependent upon "the philosophies of men." What is important to note is that both the Lutheran and the Calvinist lines, including their modern radically orthodox versions, throw themselves completely on revelation and deprive themselves of consistent philosophical theist constructs to surround their witness to revelation. Since in philosophical theisms there are means for overcoming or addressing the contradictions of "transcendent immanence" or "immanent transcendence," there are ways in the Catholic tradition (or in kinds of Protestantism which neglect or reject the Ur-Protestant witness) for "cushioning the shock" in the language of "God is dead," as heard in the Golgotha of the hymnodic tradition.

Jesus Christ: There Is No Other God

Parallel to the epistemological problems associated with Lutheran-Calvinist approaches to transcendence-immanence is the subject of Christology implied in "death of God" language and revealed again in the early chorales. Luther himself in one verse of his greatest hymn speaks of Jesus Christ as "the Lord of Hosts" — *Und ist kein and'rer Gott.* "There is no other God." Lutheran scholastic orthodoxy along with Luther himself found many ways of protecting and safeguarding his assertion. One may say: The Christian knows no other God than the one revealed in Jesus Christ. But if in the isolation of the Good Friday hymn "God himself is dead" when Jesus is dead, so in the hymn *Ein Feste Burg,* "there is no other God" than the God perceived in Jesus Christ as Lord of Hosts. The modern "death of God" theology, insofar as it attaches itself to the incarnation or to Jesus, picks up in isolation this ascription. The fate of Jesus is the fate of God; there is no other fate. Jesus dies; God dies. We are identified with Jesus: we die; God dies.

The Reformation leaders knew of the ancient heresy of Patripassianism; they knew that it was not proper to speak of God the Father suffering in the Son. This had been condemned as Sabellianism or as a form of Monarchianism, and the Protestants were not interested in buying old Christological heresies.

Yet in practice, witness to God the Father or to God the Holy Spirit has often receded far into the background, and pietist Protestantism at least has tended to celebrate Jesus to the point that this reverence became, in H. Richard Niebuhr's phrase, "a Unitarianism of the Second Person." This pietistic perversion of Trinitarianism is culturally conditioned and almost accidental. Yet there are frequent temptations toward modalism in the Protestant tradition and in this modalism Jesus Christ as God accessible, manifest, empirically present in our history, will receive first attention. Once again, because of this Christological accent, the fate of Jesus becomes the fate of God. Contemporary "death of God" theology, rejecting the metahistorical basis of Christ-talk, the cosmic screen against which the drama of Jesus was portrayed, retains Jesus. Thus it retains one authentic Protestant note and by a curious neglect of others is able to exploit an evangelical insight into a new Gospel of Christian atheism: God is dead. Jesus lives. The Word remains incarnate. Once again, when "God dies" it seems as if a Protestant is on the scene.

Faith as the Creator of Divinity

Protestantism has accented what Przywara called "soteriological anthropocentrism."[10] Isolating those features in Pauline and Augustinian thought which stressed personal individual salvation, it concentrated its energies on the subject of faith. Having ruled out both speculative philosophy and human merit as avenues of access to God, the earliest Protestants found themselves relying entirely on faith. This faith was intensely theocentric, reliant on the promises of God in Jesus Christ, as revealed in the word of preaching, the Scripture, and the sacraments.

God is hidden, even when He reveals Himself in the suffering and dying Christ on the cross and even when He makes Himself known in His creatures, in nature and history. But man is manifest, near, and accessible. Psychological and theological witness therefore tended to unite in their expressions of curi-

---

[10] *Op. cit.*, p. 272.

osity about the believing subject. Luther was even able to speak
of faith as "the Creator of divinity in man" and, in order to suggest the intimacy of personal appropriation of revelation, could
advise, "*Glaubst du, so hast du*"; "As you believe, so you have."[11]

For Luther such comment never was to be taken in isolation
from the agency of God the revealer. But radicals in the Protestant tradition, once again by moving slightly off center, made
much of the fact that such an approach to faith rendered the
line between theology and anthropology a very narrow one
indeed. Among the left-wing Hegelians it was Feuerbach who
most consistently tried to maintain that God-talk was really
talk about man, that language of faith in a divine object
was really talk about a human subject.[12] (Curiously, the twentieth-century Protestants who speak about "the death of God"
have dealt secondarily with Feuerbach, whose witness was
actually more problematic to religious orthodoxy than Nietzche's
was. Perhaps the dramatic and relentless writing of Feuerbach,
who posed the substantial problems for later theology, would
cause his twentieth-century heirs' work to seem pale by comparison!) While Feuerbach has tended to be neglected, the idea
of faith as an illusion which erects a deity has been promoted in
our culture by Freud and his followers.

Karl Barth admitted that Feuerbach posed the nearly un-
answerable questions and framed the problems most threatening to faith. By connecting revelation with faith while
speaking in his earlier years of God as "wholly other," Barth
himself had drawn attention to man as subject, despite his
own life-long polemic against man-centered theology. Paul
Tillich, from another angle, by separating the concept of "faith"
from that of "belief," maximized the existential bearing of the
subject and minimized or ruled out a content-relation to the
object, God. The generation which followed Barth and Tillich,

[11] *Fides* is *creatrix divinitatis in nobis* (Weimar Ausgabe) 40, I; 360.
[12] Feuerbach details his view in *The Essence of Christianity* (New York:
Harper Torchbook, 1957); see Gerhard Ebeling, *Word and Faith* (Phila-
delphia: Westminster, 1963), p. 346; Barth's comment on Feuerbach is in
Protestant Thought from Rousseau to Ritschl (New York: Harper and
Row, 1959), p. 355 ff.

living in a culture in which witness to revelation was even more difficult than it had been in Barth's time and in which Tillich's kind of metaphysic was called into question, was left with man on its hands. It had to deal with Feuerbach's legacy, as it were. Curiosity about man, about his being, his faith, produced vivid material for study. God paled. Translate: "God died."

God-Forgetters as God-Killers

We can best perceive the ways in which Protestantism played into the hands of the "death of God" thinkers by detailing some features of the developing culture just mentioned. This culture, encouraged on Protestant terrain, can be characterized by words like "industrial," "technological," "scientific." It represents the fulfillment of four centuries' efforts toward secularization. Particularly through the work of Dietrich Bonhoeffer,[13] Protestants have come to regard these efforts as legitimate Christian concerns. The scientific inquirer or the industrial achiever was seen as an agent of Christ as Lord: his every advance might serve to destroy magic, superstition, false religion — each of which had enslaved people. Each advance served to bring new areas of creation under human dominion, and the mandate for such conquest lay in Scripture itself. Progressively, God was not needed in the laboratory or the legislature. Whereas once upon a time Laplace's word that he had no need for God as an hypothesis in the laboratory had been taken as a threat to Christians, in the new secular Protestantism it was taken as a joke on Laplace for having raised the issue, for having become an unwitting servant of Christian purpose. The "God of the gaps" had to go, the God who had been an "x" in human equations was no longer necessary.

Well and good. But astute people began to ask questions for which Christians were ill-prepared. What earthly good, now, is faith? Why witness to God, if addition or subtraction of His name from discussion added or subtracted nothing substantial: the scientific experiment or industrial progress worked the same way whether or not God was mixed up with the affair. If so,

[13] Bonhoeffer, *op. cit.*, p. 156 ff.

why bother to add an extraneous and retrogressive feature like "God"? Why import myth if it does not add to meaning? If "God" cannot be falsified in philosophy, can He be affirmed?

When these questions were raised, Christians fell back more and more on the empirical, on what could be known: on the Jesus of history, on the faith of the Easter community. But the critics were able to point out that the Jesus of history was quite elusive, along the lines of conventional historical inquiry. And unconventional historical inquiry inevitably located talk about Jesus in the context of talk about Jesus Christ. Christ-talk involves people in a philosophy of history, of promise and fulfillment of hope, language which was an equivalent of God-talk. At this point, Christian apologists were given two choices. They could reintroduce open God-talk, at the risk of having to face again the original questions of theodicy and the apotheosis of scientific and cultural process. Or they could shun God-talk and, in effect, become Jesus-oriented humanists inside the Christian community. If "death of God" thinkers chose the latter course, they could point out that their confréres who had opted for God-talk had failed to produce much of cognitive import during the years since the crisis of language about God had become acute.

Historically, there has been considerable variety of response to cultural change. In Great Britain and in the United States, where industrialism came early to practical-minded people, the intrusion of a sense of the "death of God" was subtle and quiet. It needed little ideological defense. In the Anglo-American orbit we find few intellectuals proclaiming the "death of God" on the scale of Feuerbach, Nietzsche, Marx, Freud. Not that there were no "god-killers" in England, for example. Charles Darwin, Charles Bradlaugh, Bertrand Russell, and George Bernard Shaw are typical prophets of post-Christianity. For Darwin or H. G. Wells, witness to a living God merely had dried up along with other obsolete and unnecessary aspects of resource for personhood. The Victorian doubters did introduce a note of agony, but their language was characteristically poetic (as in Matthew Arnold's *Dover Beach* or in Thomas Hardy's novels) and not philosophical. In the United States the "infidels" tended to be lecturers, communitarian experimenters, promoters, but rarely first-rate minds, rarely people with authentic alternative visions.

The "death of God" in American culture ordinarily occurred, as Gabriel Vahanian[14] pointed out, by means of an immanentism which claimed "God" for justification of business or national life, which identified Him with our manifest destiny, which held Him captive in our religiosity. When this occurred, only the syllabic symbol "God" remained, out of continuity with witness to a personal "Other" who judged and redeemed His people in the past. Rarely were there articulators of a godless vision to compare, for example, with a Jean-Paul Sartre in France.

But whether the path of experiencing the "death of God" in culture took a quiet, practical course as in Anglo-America or an ideological and articulate pattern as in Germany and France, the end-process was similar. To speak of the cultural "death of God," as Vahanian does, is perhaps a linguistically more apt way of putting the question than are the versions of witness which suggest that spokesmen have had access to "events" in a transcendent order. The cultural realization of the "death of God" has not occurred only on Protestant soil: we have already introduced France as a post-Christian and often godless community and France has not been characterized as a Protestant nation. But Protestants have been more eager to celebrate the "death" of the immanent God of religiosity than have Catholics; they have been more eager to see secularization and the death of the "god of the gaps" as a fulfillment of Christian purpose than have Catholics. As today's Roman Catholics come to accept these attitudes, they will no doubt share some of the Protestant tendency to veer toward "death of God" witness.

Perhaps Catholicism will have resources when such a moment comes which Protestants were unable to employ. Alfred North Whitehead has pointed out[15] that while the industrial,

---

[14] Gabriel Vahanian, *The Death of God* (New York: Braziller, 1961), pp. 144 ff., 190 ff.

[15] Alfred North Whitehead, *Adventures of Ideas* (New York: Mentor, 1955), p. 30.

scientific, nationalist world with its new quasi-religions was developing, Protestant evangelicals chose to approach that world through pietist revivalism which appealed intuitively to the heart. The clergy wavered in their appeal to constructive reason: they saw (or if at first they did not see, they permitted through their obliviousness) the development of an uninterpreted autonomous secular order. When that order became self-conscious, Protestant theology was ill-prepared to interpret it. Perhaps Roman Catholicism will be revealed to have taken a different course. Given its long preoccupation with modes of reasoning ill-adapted to an industrial-scientific age and its "siege-mentality," I for one would not be sanguine about the possibility. If my observations are correct, on this front Protestants and Catholics stand on the same ground today and new efforts to anticipate and interpret change in the light of the Christian Gospel today are thoroughly ecumenical.

The Breakdown of Symbol

Protestants pioneered in having the experience of "aloneness" in a universe where the symbolic order was breaking down, where the empirical order no longer seemed to be transparent to a transcendent "beyond." Erich Heller, in a perceptive passage relating to an early moment in Protestant history,[16] reveals how Martin Luther in this matter still belonged with his medieval fore-bearers in his sacramental discussions with the Swiss reformer Zwingli. At Marburg in 1529 these leaders of two reformist parties met to see whether they could agree about the meaning of The Lord's Supper. Luther, inheriting the essentially medieval view, insisted that the bread and the wine are the body and blood of Christ. For him, through the Word's activity, the created order was open actually to intrusion. Zwingli, as a modern and a humanist, reduced the sacrament "to the status of an allegory (as merely representing what, in itself, it is not). From then onwards the word 'merely' has been attaching itself ever more firmly to the word 'symbol,' soon gaining sufficient strength

---

[16] Erich Heller, *The Disinherited Mind* (New York: Meridian, 1959), p. 212 f.

to bring about a complete alienation between the two spheres."
Continues Heller:

> Finally a new order of things emerged. Within it the
> transcendental realm is allotted the highest honors of the
> spirit, but, at the same time, skilfully deprived of a con-
> siderable measure of reality; the mundane, on the other
> hand, is recompensed for its lowering in spiritual stature
> by the chance of absorbing all available reality and be-
> coming more "really" real than before.

The efflorescence of physical science was a positive result of
this breach. But "religion and art lost their unquestioned birth-
right in the homeland of human reality."

Later Lutheranism, despite its persistent "orthodoxy" on
sacramental teaching, tended to share the cultural fate of
Zwinglianism and more and more isolated its regard for the
sacrament from its whole view of creation and nature. The
modern Roman Catholic seems torn, too, between a practical
day-to-day vision of the created order as open to the transcendent through sacramental symbolism on one hand, and a shut-up
view on the other. Eastern Orthodoxy seems most of all to have
retained its cultural hold on the symbolistic value of sacrament
and creation. But the disintegration of symbol has complicated
"the problem of God" most of all for Protestants and has made
it difficult for them even to analyze the propositions of those
who witness to "the Living God" or "the death of God." Recovery
of God-talk must await recovery of an awareness of meaning in
the symbolic order; such awareness has progressed too slowly to
permit theologians to make detailed reply to modern atheism,
which seems only to be more consistent in its view of the sever-
ance of orders and more cocksure about the "disappearance of
the object" beyond the mundane order.

Program for Theologians

I believe the six reasons which I have cited so far help account
for the theological problem of God on Protestant soil. These have
included certain forms of epistemology ("theology of the cross"),
complications in speaking meaningfully of "transcendent" and
"immanent" orders, tendencies toward unitarianism of the Sec-

ond Person of the Trinity, accent on the subject of faith at the expense of its object, practical atheism, and the disintegration of the symbolic order. I have made nothing at all of a possibility which historic Roman Catholicism has regularly attributed to Protestantism: that its divided state and the absence of papal authority lead to chaos and irresponsibility. This attribution seems to me to be irrelevant: when someone with a sense of consistency and honesty comes to radical discovery — for example, say, when he has a cultural experience of "stumbling over the corpse of God," he is not likely to be deterred by fear of authority from expressing his claims and stating his case. It may be true that the divided state of Protestantism has encouraged experimentalism in theology and that wildly radical movements have come from this to produce witness to "the death of God." If this is true, it is probably balanced by the expressions of "freedom" on the part of those who leave what they have regarded to be authoritarian and repressive Catholic cultural settings.

Whether or not Protestantism's ultimate logic is atheist, it is true that Protestantism has been puzzled with what to do with the atheist. From Luther to Barth and Tillich there has been a certain valuation placed on his witness. Luther averred that God preferred the honest shout of the atheist to the pious prattle of the righteous. Barth suggested that the prophetic witness of the atheist was a valid judgment on human religion. Tillich placed the atheist next to the mystic as critic of institutionalized and idolatrous religiosity. Once again, Christian theologians have begun to wrestle with the problem of atheism, this time within the churches. On the face of things, "Christian atheism" seems to be such a contradiction in terms that its perseverance in the Christian community may very well be short-lived and, for that matter, public interest may be equally of short duration. Some day soon, historians may possibly be chronicling the demise of "another heresy."

The church of the past has often learned from its heretics. Eventually. It would seem to be the better part of wisdom for Christians today to examine and, if possible, learn from the most recent intrusion on their peace. The challenge of "the death of God theology" came to Protestantism not because of its gift for dealing with revelation, faith, and the empirical. Rather, it embarrassed Protestants for their inability to deal consistently with the doctrine of God, to face the problem of God in terms congruent with perceived reality in their own time, to transmit anything of cognitive value relating to the syllable "God" to non-theologians in the Christian community. As an historian, I have concentrated on the development of a problem which grew out of distortions of Protestant witness. It is impossible to carry the subject further here other than to point to the theologians with questions: If Jesus-talk is to deal with the whole of reality, so that faith in Jesus is faith in the Christ, then are you not engaging in God-talk? And, if you are engaging in God-talk, what do you mean by God? If the "death of God" theologians have performed any service in the Church, it has been this: to call Christian thinkers to note the urgency of the question and to attempt, if possible, to provide answers appropriate for life in a new day.

Reflections on Faith
and Metaphysics*

EUGENE FONTINELL

An Unfinished Parable

A people that had lived for thousands of years on an island had developed a secure and ordered society and a comprehensive vision of their place both on the island and in the world at large. The only disturbing feature was that they could see at a distance what appeared to be other islands. These islands were separated from them by treacherous waters. For centuries, the majority on the secure island argued that all attention and energy should be directed toward the interior development of their own community's life. They warned that even looking for long periods at those other islands could be dangerous. Occasionally someone who could no longer adhere to the tight code of their island would leap into the sea and strike out for one of the others. Those who ventured forth experienced different fates. Some were seen to sink rather quickly in the sea; others apparently reached one of the islands but were never heard from again.

Eventually, however, swimmers from the other islands landed on the central island. Most of these people would describe the sad state of affairs on the island which they had left and tell the central islanders how fortunate they were to have the safety

---

* Reprinted with the permission of Dr. Fontinell and Joseph Cunneen from the Winter 1966 issue of *Cross Currents*.

and security of their society. Often the outsiders would ask permission to join the central island's society; some of them eventually made great contributions to its life.

Over the generations, the central islanders built up a large store of objects that had been brought by the newcomers or had floated ashore. Some of the more enterprising islanders came to value these objects and concluded that, though the central island society had everything absolutely necessary to a full life, worthwhile things were nevertheless being produced on the other islands. From time to time, some adventurous youth would ask the leaders for permission to swim to one of the islands in order to return with knowledge and objects that might enrich the life of the central island. At first, the leader refused permission; later, a compromise was developed. Certain specially trained individuals would be permitted to venture forth but only on the condition that they be fastened to a lengthy and strong life-line. If they encountered any danger they had only to pull on the line and they would be hauled back to the safety of the central island. This plan worked well. Over the years, guarded two-way communication between the central island and the others developed. Both groups benefited.

The life-liners gradually assumed a special position. On the one hand they received a good deal of abuse from some of their fellow islanders, who thought they were introducing destructive changes, and from some of the other islanders who thought them cowardly for not leaving their home island permanently. On the other hand, they were also doubly celebrated: first, by some of their fellow islanders who admired their courage in venturing into strange lands while retaining their fidelity to the principles of their home society; second, by some of the other islanders who admired the life-liners' willingness to meet with them, listen to them, work with them and disagree with them.

In the course of time some of the life-liners became dissatisfied with their role. They felt that the life-line limited them in a number of ways. While they were able to meet with the other islanders, the life-lines prohibited them from having any meeting very far inland. Nor were they able to participate in such activities as descending into caves or climbing mountains. Yet they had learned that these activities, though often dangerous, frequently led to beneficial discoveries; in fact, many fruits of these discoveries had been communicated to the central island society.

These dissatisfied life-liners had no desire to separate themselves from the life of the central island but they did desire to participate more fully in the life of the other islands, arguing that they might thereby be enabled to contribute more to life on their own island and to the life of the other islands. They came to realize, however, that only by venturing out to the other islands without a life-line would they be able to achieve this. They had to admit, of course, that there was no guarantee that they could achieve their goal. They also knew that they would run great risks and that in all likelihood some of them would be permanently separated from their home island. In "fear and trembling," then, they went forth on the treacherous sea, aware that they would never again have that security and certainty which so formed their earlier existence. They had only the hope that they would not lose life itself.

I The Present Situation: The Catholic Context

One of the most striking phenomena of recent years has been the change that is taking place within that institution which for so long had differentiated itself from a world saturated with change by asserting its fundamental immutability. That the Roman Catholic Church is capable of change beyond the greatest expectations of friend or foe alike is now established beyond question. It is clear that Roman Catholicism has been influenced by the modern world's emphasis upon change; what remains obscure is the depth or quality of this influence. The question of how much and what kind of change is possible within Roman Catholicism has not yet been faced. There is still reasonable doubt that more than a few Roman Catholic leaders and thinkers are willing to admit change in any but the most superficial aspects of Roman Catholic structure and doctrine. Even the more liberal Catholic thinkers, particularly in the United States, assert that change cannot extend to fundamentals. We repeatedly encounter statements denying that the current renewal will affect the unchanging truths of the faith. The use of the term renewal is itself significant, because it implies that the hard core of Catholic truth is always present in its immutable state but that it can be at certain times poorly stated or improperly understood or covered over with superficia or given wrong emphasis. Almost everyone concedes that these immutable truths must be updated, adapted to the present, expressed in the language of the contemporary world; but the underlying assumption of almost all Catholic thinkers is that any such action must leave the fundamental truths untouched. Objectively, at least, nothing really essential has, will, or can change in the body of Catholic doctrine. Subjectively, of course, perception may deepen and expression improve. But Catholic truth, absolute and objective, will continue intact.

It is difficult today to bring into focus certain crucial issues within Roman Catholic thought, because often the language employed can be used to house quite opposing positions. Not too long ago, the issues were more clearly stated. Catholics defended immutable truths against the assaults of modern thinkers who were generally viewed as deficient in both intellect and character, a worldview generally accepted as orthodox Catholicism. Despite earlier individual (and relatively isolated) anticipations,[1] we can generalize that only since World War II has there arisen a new drift within Roman Catholic thinking. The first stage was marked by a more positive attitude toward the modern world and its thinkers. Though the Catholic position in theology and philosophy was basically and unchangeably true, there were some things to be learned from the non-Catholic world. Fifteen short years ago this positive (and often condescending) attitude toward things not Catholic was considered *avant garde* and daring.[2] Those of us who were studying and teaching in

---

[1] One immediately thinks of Cardinal John Henry Newman and Maurice Blondel.

[2] I recall the stir created by a CROSS CURRENTS editorial ("All is Good," Erwin W. Geissman, Fall, 1953) which merely criticized "simplistic" resolutions of human problems.

Catholic colleges during the late forties and fifties can attest the fact. In calling for a hearing for modern thought we were forced to insist, and to go to great lengths to show, that whatever we were affirming or whatever we found true in modern thought was already present in the "fullness" of Catholic tradition. When I say "forced" I do not mean against our will or even contrary to our understanding or belief, since certainly the overwhelming majority of us held this position. We were incapable then of thinking otherwise.

Then came John XXIII and Vatican II. Within a few years those dangerous attitudes and positions were "in." Ecumenism emerged. *Aggiornamento* became a cliché. Few but Evelyn Waugh still dared employ the simplistic anti-modern-world rhetoric that had been the hallmark of Catholicism. It no longer required daring to speak out publicly in favor of change, development of doctrine, learning from non-Catholic thinkers, even for free speech and freedom of thought within the Church. The "closed" Church had become the "open" Church, according to most Catholic spokesmen.

At first glance it would appear that the "liberal" Catholics of a decade ago should rejoice unreservedly, since their view of Catholicism has become dominant. Rejoicing there has been, though criticism has not ceased but intensified. Consequently, there have emerged critics of the critics who feel that, though criticism of the Church was necessary in the past, it is now puerile. Victory has been won, they seem to say. The "new breed" should stop fighting battles which have concluded favorably. The mopping up that inevitably follows a long and great struggle may be necessary, but we should not waste our energy in negative criticism of Catholicism. Let us instead proceed with the more positive task of building the Church now that a more favorable climate exists. Only malcontents will persist in finding fault with Catholicism.

I have caricatured this position a bit, but I think that basically the description is true and that those who share it are likely to grow in number. Even some of those who have led the struggle at the Council have expressed concern that criticism is now getting out of hand. Paul VI, moreover, in a number of talks has stated unequivocally that the traditional virtues of obedience and authority must not be pushed into the background in the name of some spurious freedom or novelty.

Much of the current criticism is, in fact, out of date. Some critics fail to appreciate how much change has taken place within the Roman Catholic Church. They continue to fight old battles. To this extent the caution against dwelling on former sins is well taken and we should take advantage of the freedom that now exists to bring forth positive ways of enriching the life of the Church. Unfortunately, however, the situation is more complicated. The extent and depth of the change that has taken place within Catholicism is by no means clear and unequivocal. Many of those who have ostensibly accepted the new ideas and attitudes that have emerged in the past few years do not seem fully aware of their implications. In a sense, conservative Catholics have been more perceptive concerning the modern world and its thought than have those who think of themselves as liberals. The conservatives see that you cannot traffic in new ideas without running great risks and, perhaps more important, that, to the extent new ideas are really contacted, old ideas will be changed. Further, they see that the Church cannot really remain the same if it becomes impregnated with these ideas. The liberal Catholic has, of course, a way out of this situation. He argues that change can take place in the accidentals without touching the essentials, that it is possible to maintain absolutely immutable doctrines side by side with mutable expressions and understandings of those doctrines.

This latter position, which characterizes most liberal American Catholic thinkers (and indeed most Catholics throughout the world), will, I suggest, run more and more into difficulty. It may be that theirs is the best possible interpretation of Catholicism, that while there will always be change this change will continually be limited by a hard-core of absolutely unchangeable truths and doctrines. Thus the continuing task of the theologian will be to free this unchangeable wheat from the everchanging chaff. If this is so, then in all honesty we should admit that Catholics cannot really integrate the results of the great revolutions in thought which have occurred over the last four hundred years, and in particular those of the last hundred years. My conviction, however, is this: the conservatives have more fully grasped the nature of change. We have set out on waters more treacherous than most liberals can admit. Change will in the future affect "immutable" truth.

II Faith and Metaphysics:

a) The Contemporary Context: The real measure of development and susceptibility to contemporary thought and experience is not to be found in the willingness of the Church to modify its dominant teaching on the Jews or religious liberty, or even birth control. Important as each of these may be they can all be updated without seriously threatening the underlying, allegedly immutable structure and doctrines of the Church. The challenging implications of the developmental (processive) view of reality becomes evident only when we center our attention on the general area of faith and metaphysics, which includes such specific problems as the knowledge of God, certitude, atheism and meaning. The resolution of such questions by most Catholic thinkers is rooted in a worldview fundamentally opposed to the worldview that permeates the thought patterns and experiences of the more creative thinkers of our time. This is a large assertion; it hardly admits of proof in the usual sense of the term. One cannot, I suspect, debate such large issues as "metaphysical worldview" or "the testimony of history." There are data to support all viewpoints. My concern is not to argue the superiority of contemporary metaphysics, but to stress the difference between it and traditional or classical metaphysics. Explication of a fundamental difference between the two is a more difficult task than is generally thought; I hope merely to indicate a few crucial points of divergence. The most serious obstacle in the way of this undertaking is that, though the term contemporary metaphysics is convenient, there is no clearly definable and localizable entity to which it can be applied. Contemporary metaphysics is in the process of formation; any description of it must be tentative. Nevertheless, I see what can be designated as a metaphysics emerging from a range of contemporary thinkers who are by no means in full or even basic agreement. Different as Husserl may be from Dewey, Heidegger from James, Bergson from Whitehead, they still share a world; and that world is sharply differentiated from the varied but equally unified world of Maritain and Gilson, Murray and Daniélou, de Lubac and Rahner.

The safest generalization that can be made about contemporary thinkers is that they no longer function in terms of underlying substantial essences which are able to be accidentally changed or qualified. For the contemporary man it is reality and not simply an aspect or dimension of reality which is in process. In place of a world of substantial things extrinsically related he offers a world of "fields" or constellations of focused relations. In the contemporary world, process and relation rather than structure and substance are the controlling categories. The contemporary thinker offers a world in which subject and object, subjective and objective, are derivative rather than ultimate categories.[3] Thus it is almost always misleading to apply the traditional use of these terms to their thought. Yet it is precisely these terms in which the Catholic intellectual world thinks and through which it sees and tries to accept or refute the world of modern thought. The process is akin to using a microscope to study the Milky Way.

My problem is not to prove the truth of rational metaphysics

---

[3] This is a most difficult notion to communicate since we are so deeply conditioned to interpret our experience in terms of subject and object. The overcoming of this dichotomy, however, is the aim of such thinkers as James, Dewey, Husserl and Heidegger, to name but a few. That this denial of subject and object as ultimate categories is not an esoteric philosophical theory can be seen from the importance which the existential psychologists assign to it. Cf. *Existence*, edited by Rollo May (New York: Basic Books, 1958), where both May and Ludwig Binswanger repeatedly make this point. E.g., May states: *"Existentialism, in short, is the endeavor to understand man by cutting below the cleavage between subject and object which has bedeviled Western thought and science since shortly after the Renaissance"* (p. 11, May's italics); and Binswanger: "Only . . . through the concept of being-in-the-world as transcendence has the fatal defect of all psychology been overcome and the road cleared for anthropology, the fatal defect being the theory of a dichotomy of world into subject and object" (p. 193).

over against that of realistic substantialism. My only point is that there is such a metaphysics in existence, if only in emergent form. Further, it is a reasonable reading of contemporary philosophy and science to conclude that this is gaining dominance and everything points in the direction of its becoming, willy-nilly, the way in which mankind sees and understands. Now this may in fact be a contemporary delusion; it is not impossible that despite present appearances the perennial realistic metaphysics is really perennial and that it will eventually show itself capable of assimilating the new discoveries of philosophy and science without serious modification of its basic principles. On the other hand, it is possible, and I think probable, that traditional realistic metaphysics has had its day; though it will always be necessary to account for certain of its basic insights, its world of substantial things and unchanging essences and absolutely certain knowledge of them is already in the past and irrevocably so.

If this is so, the Catholic Church may be heading for a metaphysical Galileo case. All now agree on the disaster for the Church in its having attached itself to a particular physics. It is conceivable that it invites a comparable disaster by attaching itself to a particular metaphysics. The issue, for a variety of reasons, is immensely more complicated, but the parallel is not drawn without some justification. If we were to pose the question simply as to whether the act of faith commits one to a particular metaphysics — Thomism, for example — most Catholic thinkers, including Thomists, would probably say no. Yet the overwhelming number of Christian and certainly Catholic theologians presuppose a metaphysics which, if not Thomistic, is certainly fundamentally realistic and substantialistic.[4] The contrast in the contemporary world is not really between Platonic or Aristotelian, Augustinian or Thomistic metaphysics. Despite many and important differences among these great thought

---

[4] Striking confirmation of this can be found in Claude Trestmontant's recently published *Christian Metaphysics* (New York: Sheed and Ward, 1965). Trestmontant argues "that there is *one* Christian philosophy and one only" (p. 19). The "Christian metaphysics" which he then proceeds to describe is clearly "realistic and substantialistic."

systems there is fundamental agreement. Compared with the world that emerges from modern and contemporary thought, the four great thinkers of ancient and medieval times present worlds that appear remarkably similar if not identical. Nowhere does the contrast between the classical and contemporary worlds become more crystallized than in the problem of God, specifically with reference to our knowledge of God. I believe that it will prove useful to sharpen the contrast between the traditional and contemporary viewpoints on this question and its corollaries.[5]

b) *Some Traditional Views:* As a first step in focusing the issue it might be helpful to present the recent treatment which the problem of God received in the works of two excellent Roman Catholic theologians. The first is *The Problem of God* by John Courtney Murray, S.J. (New York: Yale University Press, 1964); the second is *The Search for God* by R. W. Gleason, S.J. (New York: Sheed & Ward, 1964). Murray states that his purpose in *The Problem of God* is historical and descriptive. In great part he adheres to this plan, yet some of the most interesting parts of the work are argumentative. In these sections, he has sharpened the traditional position in such a way that its conflict with contemporary thought is most clear. In addition, the metaphysic that underlies his historical and descriptive method inevitably brings Murray into conflict with the dominant trend of contemporary thought. His metaphysical assumptions stand out most clearly in the chapter entitled "The Theological Problem; The Understanding of God." In his considera-

---

[5] There is a strong temptation at this point to enter into a long-winded apology for being so presumptuous as to attempt to handle such profound questions in so brief an article. Actually, I think that we should be well past this attitude of debilitating humility. In point of fact no one is ever adequate to such questions whether in an article, a book or a dozen books. Only the community is adequate, because it alone has a life sufficiently long to absorb and correct the partial insights of its members. The need of the moment would not seem to be for ultra-orthodox, well-rounded, indefinitely qualified and eminently safe restatements of traditional positions. Rather what seems desperately needed is some free-wheeling hypothesizing on questions that are tearing out the insides of an increasing number of Catholics who fervently desire to be faithful to the demands which contemporary thought and life make upon them and at the same time not to separate themselves from participation in the Church.

tion of the formulation of the Nicene Creed, Murray is led to conclude "that behind the Athanasian rule lay the universal patristic conviction that, to put the matter in technical terms, a realist epistemology and ontology are implicit in the conception of the word of God which the Scriptures exhibit" (p. 43). The realistic metaphysics that Murray finds implicit in the Scriptures and the Creed seems to embody two distinct but inseparable features. These two features are included in the following passage:

> These affirmations [of the Old and New Testaments] are not a matter of religious experience but of ontology. these two categories. Creator and creature, are classifications of being. They define things that are and that are radically distinct in the order of substance (p. 43).

Murray seems to maintain that the Scriptures are not reducible to the religious experience of the sacred writers and that the world is a world of distinct and definable substances. The first question is whether these two assertions must be affirmed or denied jointly. Though he does not explicitly say so, Murray's answer would seem to be yes. Throughout he seems to imply that the only alternative to a realistic metaphysics is a destructive and superficial subjectivism.[6]

From the perspective of the believer, the question is, to what extent is his religious belief inseparable from the metaphysics which Murray finds in the Creed and Scripture?

> In the adjective *homoousion* the Nicene problem of God finds its definitive answer. The answer is given, as it had to be given, not in the empirical categories of experience, the relational category of presence, or, even, the dynamic categories of power and function but in the ontological category of substance, which is a category of being. Nicaea did not describe; it defined (p. 45).

---

[6] Prescinding a moment from the strictly religious question, it should be noted that while thinkers such as James, Dewey or Whitehead might be called realists insofar as they deny that everything is a one-sided projection of the human subject, they cannot be called realists if one means by the term that the world is structured according to unchangeable essences or independent substantial things. All I am concerned to do at the moment is to point out that we can no longer settle philosophical (or theological) issues in the more simplistic terminology of subjectivity and objectivity.

If Murray is simply giving an historical description of the understanding characteristic of those who formulated the Creed, I believe that there can be little argument with this statement. His implication, however, is more far-reaching and serious — he holds that the mode of understanding and the form of expression which the Fathers used is final. This becomes evident in his treatment of the kind of development of doctrine which is manifest in the Creed. Murray contends that "it was not new, and it was new." The *sense* found in the Scriptures was not new but the mode of understanding was new.

> The transition is from a mode of understanding that is descriptive, relational, interpersonal, historical-existential, to a mode of understanding that is definitive, explanatory, absolute, ontological. The alteration in the mode of understanding does not change the sense of the affirmation, but it does make the Nicene affirmation new in its form (p. 46).

Let us prescind from the epistemological difficulties in a position that holds for a new mode of understanding which "does not change the sense of the affirmation." I simply wish to call attention to the two levels of immutability which Murray affirms: first, the immutable "sense of the affirmation" of the Scriptures; second, the immutability of the mode of understanding in which the Creed is grasped by the Fathers. Murray seems to hold that while there is development of doctrine, it is legitimate only within highly circumscribed limits, limits which in the instance of the Creed have already been reached. He holds that the Creed is the expression of an "orthodox Center" which avoids the two fallacies of archaism and futurism. The fallacy of archaism is characterized by "the rejection of the notion that Christian understanding of the affirmation of faith can and indeed must grow, at the same time that the sense of the affirmations remains unaltered" (p. 48). On the other hand, "the futurist fallacy rests on the notion that the affirmations of Christian faith can never have a final sense. They are constantly subject to reinterpretation in terms of any sort of contemporary philosophical thought" (p. 49). He later states: "The *homoousion* represents a limit in the understanding of the faith. As there is no stopping short of it on peril of archaist imprecision in the faith, so there is no going beyond it on peril of futurist adultera- tion of the faith" (p. 50).

Murray recognizes that to speak of "the development of doc- trine" can be misleading — "one might better speak of growth in understanding of the primitive affirmations contained in the New Testament revelation" (p. 51).

> The question is, what is legitimate development, what is organic growth in the understanding of the original deposit of faith, what is warranted extension of the primitive discipline of the Church, and what, on the other hand, is accretion, additive increment, adulteration of the deposit, distortion of true Christian discipline (p. 53).

The position has great force. Yet, I suggest, in embracing it, Murray has inextricably tied his interpretation to the old meta- physics, and that it is incompatible with contemporary meta- physics. If he has expressed the sole orthodox interpretation of development of doctrine, it would seem but honest for Roman Catholics to acknowledge the fundamental unacceptability of modern views of process and development. These views do not permit division of reality into an unchanging essential or sub- stantial part and a changing unessential or accidental part. But this seems to be exactly what must be held if Murray's position is to be maintained. Conversely, if Murray's presupposed meta- physics is no longer viable, if man can no longer see within its terms, Roman Catholicism seems doomed to being little more than an antiquity, a museum piece happily preserved within the modern world.

Murray seems to rule out the need that even the fundamental Christian mysteries have to be continually reworked in keeping with the development of human experience and human thought. Again, his metaphysics controls his theology for it does not allow him to admit the kind of development in human nature called for in contemporary thought and experience. Of course Murray does not deny change or process or development — no serious thinker ever really has. The question is whether change as understood by the contemporary thinker can be assimilated to change as admitted by Murray and those who share his metaphysical viewpoint. I do not believe that it can be, since the change which has captivated the contemporary world is a change which goes to the very root of being, a change from which nothing is excluded. Here, of course, is where even the most liberal Roman Catholic thinker tends to back off: such change seems necessarily chaotic and destructive.

A contemporary developmental view of man asserts much more than the gradual realization of a potential nature which is given at the outset. Such a view will concede continuity while strongly insisting on novelty. Though the *new* man and *new* world are both similar and dissimilar to the old, it denies that these features can be accounted for by positing certain absolutely unchanging principles which are capable of indefinite accidental modification. Admittedly, in this emerging view of man and the world there is much that is vague, unfinished, and inadequate. Yet, those who are advancing it insist that the data with which they are dealing cannot be accounted for by a metaphysical dualism which explains both man and reality in terms of changing and unchanging principles. A developed explanation of why such a dualism is unacceptable is beyond the scope of this article. It should be noted, however, that such an explanation would demand confrontation with the contention of a major strand of contemporary thought which holds that essences are fundamentally relational. Such a position retains continuity without maintaining a static metaphysical substructure. Thus novelties are able to emerge which are more than particularized expressions of eternal and immutable essences. Essences themselves can be novel and changing as a result of the continuous transactions taking place within the relational continuum. It must be emphasized that while novelty does not in itself threaten continuity, it does prevent us from ever claiming to know the ultimate principles of reality.

Such a radical developmental theory has, of course, grave implications for Christianity and in particular for Roman Catholicism which has long defended the absolutely unchanging in man, the world and religion.

There can be no doubt that Murray represents the overwhelming Roman Catholic consensus in holding for some dimension of absolutely unchanging doctrine. He has the weight
of tradition behind him and also a reflective, finely developed
and formidable metaphysics and theology. Anyone who finds
this position unacceptable is at a decided disadvantage since he
is not likely at this moment in history to have an equally developed metaphysics and theology to replace the one that has
served so long. Such a critic is forced to fall back on possibilities,
hypotheses and suggestions — and that is exactly what I in-
tend ultimately to do.[7]

Murray is undoubtedly reacting against a superficial, a-his-
torical attachment to modern thought. It is just as easy, I concede, to fall into an unreflective pro-modern position as it is to
fall into its opposite. Understandably Murray wishes to occupy
a middle ground free from the excesses of the static right and
the processive left. Most of us have the same desire, since no
one likes to think that he is onesided, obsessed with only one
dimension of an issue or only one set of factors. Yet the center
itself is relative, and the center in the thought of 325 is not the
center in the thought of 1967. Even within Roman Catholicism
it would be hard to find any reputable thinker who would deny
all development of doctrine. Most would be quite happy to
stand with Murray on his theological center. I suggest, however,
that his center is no longer the true center: world thought has
moved so far to the left that Murray's center is the only intellectually tenable right. All this is in no way proves that

---

[7] A crucial need within Roman Catholicism is to avoid closing out such
hypothesizing. Undoubtedly much of it will be superficial, imprecise and,
in that case, shortlived. But if we have learned anything from the way in
which human thought develops it is that only by permitting a certain
"wildness" of thought can the community bring forth its creative thinkers.
Roman Catholicism, particularly over the last four hundred years, has paid
a high price for its suppression of hypotheses in the dearth of creative
thinkers who have emerged from and continued living within the Church.
To ask people to criticize or think creatively only when they have a
completely developed position capable of meeting immediately every
objection that orthodoxy can pose is to ask the impossible. A thinker of
Teilhard's caliber produces a body of thought shot through with limitations, inadequacies and errors. What can much lesser minds hope to achieve?

Murray's position is wrong: it merely places him in relation to contemporary thought and suggests the possibility of a new center which might resemble what he has called the "futurist fallacy," which asserts that the affirmations of Christian faith "are constantly subject to reinterpretation in terms of . . . contemporary philosophical thought."

Murray upholds change in understanding but not in sense; let us suppose that this describes the right. We might then designate as left a position that denies continuity of thought or experience and holds that at every moment every individual simply makes of Scriptures and doctrine and reality anything he wants. A center position then might attempt to acknowledge the need for continuity of thought and experience while leaving room for a novelty which, though never completely and totally new, would include what have traditionally been referred to as the essentials as well as the accidentals of doctrine. This center would attempt to take into account the view that all thought and experience are historically and culturally conditioned; at the same time it would attempt to avoid both the substance-accident dualism of traditional metaphysics and a superficial historicism or cultural relativism. I am not prepared to prove that such a position is reconcilable with Christian experience but I do believe it rash to rule out the possibility. Murray tends to do so, however. He maintains that only a lack of historical scholarship can explain the continued existence of Harnack's thesis that "the Church of the early centuries reinterpreted the Christian faith in terms of contemporary philosophies" (p. 54). The point is well taken if Murray means that there is no counterpart for the *homoousion* to be found in Hellenic philosophy or that the Creed cannot be reduced to Hellenic thought. He does concede, however, "that in the *homoousion* the Fathers of Nicea christianized Hellenism in the single sense that they sanctioned the ontological mode of conception characteristic of the Hellenic mentality" (p. 55). This concession is much more important than Murray seems to think, for it implies that the Christian doctrine expressed in the Creed was conditioned by the mentality of the time in which it was expressed. What is to prevent future Christians from expressing doctrine in accordance with the mode of conception characteristic of their age? Only, I believe, the assumption that the Hellenic mentality is equivalent to human mentality and is not subject to change in principle — and this is precisely the assumption which underlies Murray's position.

Though it is much more in the background, this same assumption permeates Gleason's *The Search for God.* It is implicit, I believe, in his comments on man's knowledge of God. Gleason states: "Catholic theology maintains that man must *know* through reason that God exists before he arrives at faith" (p. 124). Later he adds an authoritative element to this when he says: "The First Vatican Council has made it clear that one can come to know the existence of God by reason, and that this knowledge is a certain knowledge" (p. 170). Gleason does not argue this position so much as he assumes it. He is quick to avoid any interpretation of this doctrine which would attach it inseparably to the Five Ways or to any particular proof. Roman Catholic doctrine minimally asserts "that there is open to man by natural reason, unaided either by grace or by faith, the possibility of establishing with certitude that God exists" (p. 171). As Gleason well knows, the controversy concerning knowledge of the existence of God does not center solely or even primarily on any particular proof or proofs but extends to the very possibility of such knowledge. The overwhelming majority of contemporary thinkers denies this possibility. This, in itself, of course, settles nothing, since in some future time as in times past the majority of "contemporary" thinkers might affirm the possibility of knowing by reason the existence of God.

My concern is not with the relative merits of the arguments for or against the possibility of knowing God's existence but is restricted to the following question: Can the Church make as an article of faith that which in itself is a philosophical conclusion, namely that unaided reason can know the existence of God? I think not. Philosophical questions, just as much as scientific questions, must be settled by rational arguments and only by rational arguments. The Church, whether viewed as the totality of its members, or as the pope, or as the hierarchy in council, has no special epistemological or metaphysical competence. There can be, needless to say, no objection to Catholic philosophers or theologians arguing loud and long for the possibility of knowing God through reason, but they must be willing to stand on the strength of their arguments. After all, there is something distasteful in saying that we are glad to enter open and rational discussion of God's existence but regardless of what emerges in the discussion we already know the answer.

A continuing irony in this dispute is that many Catholics, to say nothing of Christians in general, do not find arguments for God's existence compelling. Most contemporary Catholic thinkers attempt to account for the fact with a distinction utilized by Gleason: ". . . while the Five Ways prove, they do not necessarily persuade" (p. 233). Since Gleason makes this distinction within the context of his discussion of Pascal and Newman he appears to be operating on the assumption that you can have an argument which compels the intellect but not the total person. Such an assumption is understandable for someone operating within the thought patterns of the seventeenth or even the nineteenth century. But it should be intolerable to a twentieth-century personalist such as Gleason since it involves a fragmentation of the self which personalism (and modern thought in general) forcefully rejects. Indeed, the very features of Pascal's and Newman's thought which remain compelling are those which stress the lived rather than the abstract intellective dimensions of man's experience. Gleason seems to juxtapose a rather unimaginative traditional theological position with a perceptive phenomenological and existential one. The concluding paragraphs of his study exemplify what one is tempted to describe as intellectual schizophrenia. First, the nod to tradition:

> It is to be hoped that this study may make more clear the teaching of the Church concerning the fact of the possibility of arriving at a knowledge of God through reason, and how this knowledge is arrived at by many who are unaware of the formal proofs for the existence of God. *Beyond doubt,* there is a natural pre-philosophic awareness

of God in man which seems to be the necessary, latent "matter" for the "form" of all the logical demonstrations for the existence of God (p. 289, italics added).

There immediately follow two paragraphs which manifest sensitivity to the tentativeness and searching that characterize the contemporary scene:

> In completing his discussion of the ways of the practical intellect, Maritain, like de Lubac, includes the testimony of the friends of God. Both men would seem to imply that, no matter what convictions a man has reached through his own efforts, some distrust remains. He is curious to know the feelings of his fellows, *uncertain* that his own conclusions are valid. Although they are certainly true insofar as he can determine, who is to say that his entire approach, his intellectual equipment, are not faulty? By the same token, having heard the testimony of his comrades, some *doubt may remain*. Who is to say that judgments of the entire human order have any objective validity?
>
> *Perhaps* the answer lies in the very fact that man can have such doubts. As Marechal put it, you cannot know a limit without surpassing it. *Perhaps* man's very striving for absolute objectivity, *perhaps* his very mistrust of the entire human order, *signals* the existence of the Divine (p. 290, italics added).

Murray recognizes that the ability of reason to affirm the existence of God is "formally philosophical," but says that it is also "of vital religious import." As he sees the issue:

> It concerns the statute of reason in religion. If reason has no valid statute in religion, it follows that religion has no reasonable status in human life. Therefore it is unreasonable for a man to be religious. The reasonable man is the atheist (p. 75).

Either reason leads to theism or it leads to atheism. The possibility that reason leads to neither theism nor atheism is not considered, though Murray is, of course, aware that since Kant such a position has been philosophically respectable. It is quite understandable that in such a short work Murray had to telescope his arguments and conclusions. Nevertheless he seems deliberately to have sharpened his points, even at the risk of oversimplification. This has, I believe, decided value. Any argument or viewpoint can be qualified endlessly, and, though to some extent such refining of fundamental positions is continually necessary, a proliferation of qualifications so blurs the issues that what emerges is "a night in which all cows are black."

Most contemporary thinkers hold that reason can neither prove nor disprove the existence of God. It can, however, be misleading to juxtapose this conclusion with Murray's, because the basic conflict must again be sought in the underlying metaphysical positions. Murray is quite consistent when he argues that if reason does not lead to God, it is unreasonable to be religious — given his particular metaphysical framework. Murray presupposes a world rationally ordered and structured; man in that world is characterized by the faculty of reason and so is capable of reaching the principles of order in that world. As a consequence, if God is the fundamental principle of unity and order in the world, He must be discoverable by reason; and, if reason does not discover such a principle, He does not exist. Either theism or atheism.

The greatest obstacle in any dispute concerning reason is the wide range of meanings attached to the term. Nothing is more discouraging to students of philosophy than to discover that though a Murray and a Dewey may both use the same term, only a grasp of the fundamental principles of their philosophies makes it possible to discern both the similarity and dissimilarity of meanings. Only a detailed history of its use would adequately clarify the changes, shadings and nuances which attach to the term reason.[8] Two generalizations can be made, however. First, in the tradition which Murray represents, reason has a broad meaning and is often used as the equivalent of human

---

[8] This change took place as all such changes in terminology and intellectual categories take place — not as the result of conscious or deliberate effort but as the result of a variety of intellectual, historical and cultural factors. Romanticism, it might be noted, emerged as a reaction against those rationalisms which accompanied this delimitation of the term reason. Existentialism, the twentieth-century form of romanticism, has been labeled "irrationalism." That label is misleading, however, since the existentialist positively affirms the concrete richness of the human being over against any philosophy which appears to overemphasize reason.

nature. Second, from the seventeenth century on the term has become more and more restricted and often refers to function or set of functions among other functions performed by man. The prototype for reason in the modern sense tends to be a "scientific reason," which embodies fairly precise presuppositions and procedures, but is not the equivalent of human nature.

In contemporary language, therefore, I think it possible to say that a man of reason is not a reasonable man. By a "man of reason" we would understand someone who attempts to live solely by the results of the functions of reason. The "reasonable man" would be someone who recognizes the importance and indispensability of reason, who would never act in clear opposition to the conclusions of reason, but who at the same time recognizes other dimensions of experience as equally human. He would see, for example, that aesthetic experience enriches human existence but is not reducible to rational experience. On these terms it is conceivable that one reasonable man might be a theist and another reasonable man an atheist. Both would concede that reason alone cannot settle the question of God's existence and they would also concede that man must live in accordance with commitments that go beyond reason, at least the reason of the particular moment.

While Murray would argue, and quite persuasively, "that atheism is never the conclusion of any theory, philosophical or scientific. It is a decision, a free act of choice that antedates all theories" (p. 95), he will not concede that such is also the case with theism. Thus atheism involves fundamental irrationality but theism does not. In this, he represents a form of rationalism which has long characterized Catholic thought. This rationalism, of course, must be differentiated from one that attempts to exclude faith and reduce all mystery to reason. Catholic rationalism affirms both faith and mystery but insists that they are grounded in reason, though not accounted for by reason.

III Atheism: A Non-Speculative Consideration

Closely bound up with the charge of irrationality which the Catholic thinker raises against atheism is the even more serious charge of meaninglessness. "The question as to whether or not human existence is meaningful," according to Gleason, "depends ultimately upon the existence or non-existence of God" (p. 121). The conclusions drawn by Murray and Gleason follow with a kind of logical necessity within the framework of abstract thought. The conclusions are less compelling, however, if one focuses on the lived experience of human beings. It is not a question here of substituting romantic irrationalism for a rational view of man. Rather, it is to acknowledge what is perhaps the most important fruit of contemporary phenomenology, existentialism and pragmatism, a truth expressed with deceptive concision by William James — "life is more than logic." It is the controlling insight, principle and assumption of the late Ignace Lepp's work, *Atheism in Our Time* (New York: Macmillan, 1963).

Lepp is very much aware of the existential gap between the believer and the atheist but he refuses any kind of reductionism as an explanation: belief cannot be reduced to psychological aberration — nor can unbelief. "Neither belief nor unbelief can be adequately explained by bad faith" (p. 4).

Lepp writes about atheism with an ease and non-apologetic grace remarkable for any Christian, particularly one who is a former Marxist and atheist. A Roman Catholic and a practicing psychotherapist, he has successfully avoided the conversion syndrome of overreaction against a position which he has left. Lepp's continued awareness of the positive and human aspects of his early atheism enables him to speak in a manner eminently fair to both atheist and Christian. It is the best available introduction to dialogue between atheist and believer. The reason is that Lepp makes a great effort to clear away the peripheral features of atheism, and indirectly of Christianity, thereby preparing the way for a much fuller confrontation between the two. He permits neither party to fall back on some extrinsic or psychological explanation of why the other is what he is. Lepp, given his profession, is more aware than most that there are neurotic atheists as well as neurotic believers. But he quite properly insists that to characterize either belief or unbelief by neuroticism is to avoid encountering either in its strongest form.

One reason for Lepp's success is that he has made an existential study of atheists rather than theoretical study of atheism. Since he draws heavily upon experience, direct and indirect, he admirably avoids "explaining" or, more accurately, "explaining away" atheists. What emerge are perceptive descriptions of flesh-and-blood atheists. Though Lepp draws heavily on case studies, his gift for descriptive phenomenology is most notable; the case studies are employed to illustrate not isolated individuals but representative atheists such as Marxist, rationalist and existentialist.

Lepp's forthrightness and honesty are apparent at the outset when he says that "it seemed only right that, before submitting others to his method of psychological analysis, he ought, first of all, to exercise it on himself" (p. 11). He begins with a "preliminary chapter" on "The Atheist That I Was." This chapter alone makes the book worthwhile since it undermines the conventional Christian view of atheists. Consider, for example, the proofs for God's existence. As an atheist Lepp studied these and in his philosophy class received the highest mark in an examination on them even though as a known Communist he was examined very closely. Few Christians would be surprised or shocked to learn that as an atheist Lepp rejected these proofs, that his experience led him to conclude that these proofs "prove nothing to one who does not have faith." Rather it is his assertion that he had no interest or concern in the "God-hypothesis," that will bewilder the majority of Christians. "A religious person," Lepp tells us, "finds it very difficult to understand why atheists fail to ask certain metaphysical questions which he holds to be of the first order of importance" (p. 8). Yet, according to him, "Never in the course of my ten years as a Communist did I experience any of the 'metaphysical unrest' that is, according to believers, the common lot of thinking humanity" (p. 23).

Perhaps even less comprehensible to the Christian is Lepp's lack of interest in personal immortality — "Even when I awaited death in a Nazi concentration camp, the problem of life after death did not bother me at all" (p. 19). He goes on to say that "insofar as an understanding of a past psychic state is possible, I think I can resolutely affirm that the hope of a personal immortality did not enter into my revolutionary optimism" (p. 20).

Probably most difficult of all for Christians to understand is how one who did not believe in either God or immortality could still speak of "revolutionary optimism" or purpose. Yet Lepp in referring to his death states: "But it was impossible for me to admit that it had no purpose, that all would be reduced to nothingness" (p. 20). I think that it is fair to say that, theoretically at least, most Christians and in particular Catholics, cannot understand commitment to values and purposes unless this is tied up with "saving one's soul." Yet even after he converted to Catholicism Lepp did not find in personal immortality a motive for his actions. True, as he says, "Since I have become a Christian, I obviously believe in eternal life in general, and I hope for it personally" (p. 20). Nevertheless,

> After twenty years as a Christian, I see no instance where my behavior has been motivated by considerations concerning the future lot of my soul. It is true that when I endeavor, in terms of my limited means, to contribute to the creative work of God and the Incarnation of the Word in the history of the world, faith and hope of an eternal life are implicit in my actions. But I do not act to *merit* such a life, nor am I motivated by fear of losing it (p. 21).

IV *Faith Without Certitude: Some Possibilities*

Lepp has properly located the crisis of faith for contemporary man. He quite correctly notes that "it is not on rational grounds but rather on grounds of value, that educated men today take their stand for or against religion" (p. 132). Catholics have long assumed that atheism necessarily involves nihilism. As Lepp perceptively stated: "Believers find atheism in the name of value the most incomprehensible. . . . That men can refuse the faith because it does not demand enough and does not propose a sufficiently elevated ideal, this still rings as a scandalous paradox to almost all Christian ears" (p. 159). Whatever speculative arguments can be marshalled to show that atheism is inconsistent with meaningful value-commitment, it is beyond dispute that men who consider themselves atheists do indeed commit themselves to numerous values. The issue between atheism and theism cannot be resolved in the speculative order since both positions, when consciously affirmed, involve a commitment of self which includes dimensions or factors not reducible to reason.

The religious question must be shifted from a framework dominated by thought categories to one characterized by life categories. No Catholic spokesman would explicitly affirm the priority of thought over life but it is not unjust to say that Catholic history since scholasticism has been unduly concerned with the rational elements in religion. However understandable this imbalance may be, the mark it has left upon the Catholic community is presently undesirable. Some will argue that in recent years Catholics have acknowledged their rationalistic excess and are well on the way toward correcting it. They might adduce the widespread appeal of certain forms of existentialism and personalism with their emphasis upon lived experience rather than abstract thought. Yet, as I said earlier, these new modes of experience are perhaps being bought too cheaply. Ready though most Catholic thinkers are to concede the need for change in terminology and concepts and the need for a greater emphasis upon life and experience, they still hold out for at least a minimal rational superstructure that, grounded in the changelessness of being, is impervious to the vicissitudes of life. This juxtaposition of the traditional emphasis upon the rational and immutable and the contemporary emphasis upon the existential and developmental cannot, I feel, long be maintained. The reason is not a conflict of ideas — men have always been able to live lives which affirm conflicting ideas. There is, rather, a conflict in modes of life which men can only for a short time sustain.

These conflicting modes of life can be described simply: The Catholic mode of life is characterized by certainty and the contemporary mode by uncertainty.[9] Even the most liberal Catholic

---

[9] It may appear that I am beating a dead horse, since more and more Catholics are willing to admit that their claim "to have the truth" has been excessively stated and too simply understood. The most conservative of Catholics will admit that in the past the Church has affirmed as certain

still claims that there are at least a few things that are certain — and absolutely certain. The overwhelming thrust of contemporary thought, experience and life, on the other hand, has been away from absolutes and certainty. Now if Roman Catholicism is inseparable from absolute certainty, however minimal, we must face two unsettling implications. First, the Roman Catholic stands in a privileged position, free from the doubt and anguish which characterize contemporary life. Second, as soon as a Roman Catholic feels compelled to surrender all claims to absolute certainty he loses his identity as Catholic.

Catholics are not held to a philosophy of absolute certainty by either simple-minded authoritarianism or antiquarian nostalgia. They are held to absolutes, I believe, primarily because, like Murray, they see as the *only* alternative subjectivism, relativism and nihilism. Catholic thinkers pose for themselves the wrong question: "Does nihilism logically follow from a denial of absolute certainty?" Rather, the question is, "Do men in fact lead meaningful lives in the absence of absolute certainty?"

This latter question is settled in the affirmative not by argumentation but by the existence of such men as Albert Camus who, having looked full on the terrifying faces of doubt, despair and nihilism, have refused to succumb. Anyone of us could name others — some famous, some unknown, some reflective, some unreflective — who live lives of great meaning in the absence of certitude and often in the absence of any awareness of God. Catholics often respond to this fact by saying that the good atheist is really, deep down a Christian whether he knows it or not. Thus, with the good atheist baptized, God remains useful. After all, of what use would He be if man could be man without Him? A possible response, of course, may be that God is of no use whatever and that is why He is God.

Can Catholicism surrender its traditional claims to absolute certitude without surrendering its meaning, identity and fundamental mission? I believe that it can and must. Further, I sug-

---

much that turned out to be wrong. To say this, however, is to say that there is a trend within Catholicism to narrow the limits of absolute certitude. The trend may lead to acceptance of uncertainty on the contemporary scale. But it has not yet done so. The horse is still alive.

gest that it may well be that only in this way will it move toward
a more adequate awareness of its task. Of course, neither I nor
anyone else can know with certainty that the Catholic Church
will survive in its present form or in another. We can, however,
believe in its survival; but unless we are fatalists we will also
believe that the way in which its members live will have profound effects upon the quality of that survival. Since the religious life of a community cannot be isolated from its dominant
thought patterns, reflection will always play a role in this life.
This has been particularly true of the Catholic tradition in
Christianity and it has been one of its strengths. My criticism
of Catholicism is not that it has a long history of faith permeated by metaphysics, but that since the late Middle Ages there
has been a greater and greater tendency to freeze the unlimited
mystery and possibilities of the faith within a particular metaphysic. It would be foolish to say that this metaphysical under-
pinning has been completely without merit for Catholicism in
particular and Christianity in general, but it is also foolish and
even dangerous to suggest that this relationship is incapable of
radical transformation.

A vital and articulate faith cannot be completely independent
of metaphysics. Indeed, there is an implicit metaphysic in the
most unreflective faith as there is in the most primitive life. Nor
do I maintain that every metaphysics is equally apt for illumination and development of the Christian faith. It is no simple task,
however, to judge which metaphysics are viable within the Christian faith. Only by permitting the widest range of reflection and
practice can we discover those which impede and those which
further Christian life.

Let us concretize the problem by offering some possibilities
for a Christian faith freed from the traditional characteristics of
certitude and realistic metaphysics.[10] My controlling hypothesis
is that faith does not give knowledge about God or man or the

---

[10] It will be obvious to those familiar with contemporary thought that
there is little that is startlingly original in my suggestions. I believe,
however, that to attempt to trace out and document each aspect of my
position would result in a delay and a detour but would not substantially
affect the central points I am trying to make.

world but that it may give illumination, direction and meaning to human life. Religious or theistic faith would be the encounter or at least the affirmation of the possibility of an encounter between God and man. Since the possibility of self-deception is ever present, there is no way for the believer to free himself totally from doubt and uncertainty. It is this very characteristic, however, which gives to faith its distinctive quality: having reflectively considered the possibility that his belief may be nothing more than a psychological projection of himself, the believer is willing literally to stake his life on his belief. The believer could not, of course, *know* that his belief was merely a projection of himself and continue to believe. Precisely because this issue cannot be resolved definitively one way or the other, belief cannot be identified with blind unreflectiveness any more than it can be identified with rational certitude.

In maintaining that faith does not give knowledge, I do not mean that developed faith would not embody knowledge in some way. It is impossible for the believer to avoid incorporating the concepts and categories of the thought of his time; historically, he always has. The crucial difference is the role that such concepts and categories play within the framework of faith. In the view I am hypothesizing, they never *inform* us about anything; they rather serve as limited and relatively inadequate symbols of unknowable and inexpressible mysteries. Since, however, such symbols are necessary for the deepening and enriching of human life, they play an indispensable role. It is important to note here, of course, that while concepts and categories play a necessary role in the life of faith, no particular set of concepts or categories is necessary. This is why a dynamic faith can always surrender whatever knowledge it might have employed. Inasmuch as the purpose of faith is life and not knowledge, the thought categories involved must always be judged in terms of the quality of life that they produce in the believer and not in terms of their abstract epistemological adequacy.

Catholic thinkers who are reluctant to speak of religious language as totally symbolic seem to fear that doing so is equivalent to calling religious language subjective. It should be borne

in mind, however, that with the surrender of objectivism even
in science it is becoming increasingly difficult to maintain a
sharp dichotomy between a symbol which is primarily if not
exclusively subjective and knowledge which is primarily if not
exclusively objective. It is now being suggested that even scientific knowledge is symbolic in that we no longer have a one-to-
one correspondence between mind and reality but rather a continuing transaction in which man's knowledge is a pathway to a
more adequate relationship with reality.[11] Even on these terms
it is still crucial to distinguish faith and knowledge, however,
since the latter still retains a mode of verification not open to the
former. It is in this sense that faith is said to give meaning
rather than knowledge. This does not mean that faith may not involve and be responsive to the best knowledge of the time; it
certainly should be so responsive. It will employ this knowledge
symbolically; and for this very reason faith can never be exhausted by nor definitively committed to any knowledge. The
same faith, as a result, can continue to vitalize and energize men
living in radically different worlds and times and also can sur-

---

[11] There are immense difficulties in articulating these transactions, but
the tradition of American thought, proceeding from Peirce and James and
developed by Dewey and Mead, has highlighted the inadequacy of a
correspondence or spectator theory of knowledge. See in particular Dewey's
Experience and Nature and Mead's *The Philosophy of the Act.*
The rejection of scientific knowledge as purely objective is by no means
a peculiarity of American pragmatism. Cf. Hannah Arendt's *Between Past
and Future* (New York: Meridian Books, 1963), where she states: "The
nineteenth-century opposition of the natural and historical sciences, together
with the allegedly absolute objectivity and precision of the natural scientists, is today a thing of the past. The natural sciences now admit that with
the experiment, testing natural processes under prescribed conditions, and
with the observer, who in watching the experiment becomes one of its
conditions, a 'subjective' factor is introduced into the 'objective' processes
of nature" (p. 48). Corroborative evidence can also be found in contemporary science in its more speculative dimensions. P. W. Bridgman in *The
Logic of Modern Physics* (New York: Macmillan, 1960), states: "Closely
connected with the sharper analysis of the operational structure of our
concepts, we may expect in the future also a closer analysis of our
inventions. This will take the form of a search for new physical facts
which shall give to our inventions the character of physical reality. In
case prolonged search fails to disclose such phenomena (as is probably
now the case with the field concept of electrodynamics), we must then
find some way of embodying explicitly in our thinking the fact that we
are dealing with pure inventions and not realities" (pp. 225–226). Cf.

render the knowledge that men of a particular time associated with the doctrines of faith. The process has, to some extent, been recognized within the Church, as current Biblical interpretations attest. There is still a conviction, however, that a core of knowledge about man and God, if not the world, escapes the conditions of history and culture. This leads to a certain irony, for many who would readily concede that the Church has been misled by too great a dependence on Aristotelian metaphysics feel that the way out is to return to the Scriptures where Christian knowledge is to be found in its pristine form. The way back draws upon the tools of cultural and historical criticism, but the assumption is that what results is the discovery of a transcendent eternal verity rather than the experience of a particular encounter in history between God and man. It further assumes that we then possess that knowledge, however minimal, that God wants us to have. This is another manifestation of an unhealthy dualism, since it tends to make all other knowledge relatively superfluous. The faith-knowledge distinction which I have suggested avoids such a dualism since it refers to two necessary and indispensable modes of human experience both of which are orientated to the one world and one God.

I do not minimize the radical nature and serious implications of the change which I have suggested in Catholic understanding of and relationship to the Scriptures. Nor do I imagine that any hypothesis that I advance does not demand extensive development and refinement. From a crudely pragmatic standpoint, however, it would be well for the Church not to rule out all explanations of the role of Scripture except those which make knowledge-claims for the Word of God. As one bit of knowledge after another must be surrendered in view of new experience

---

also *The Nature of Physical Reality, A Philosophy of Modern Physics* (New York: McGraw-Hill, 1950), where Henry Margenau says: "According to the foregoing analysis the real world comprises all valid constructs and that part of Nature which stands (or stood, in the wider sense, which includes historical reality) in epistemic correlation with them" (p. 229). The point is made most simply and succinctly by Werner Heisenberg who asserts that the "ideal of a science which is completely independent of man (i.e., completely objective) is an illusion" (cited by May, *op. cit.*, p. 26).

and insights, the "Scripture gives knowledge" advocate retreats to a gradually diminishing base of knowledge. Consequently, it becomes more and more difficult to maintain any kind of "revelation as knowledge" interpretation of the sacred writings. At this moment it is by no means beyond the argument that there is no knowledge content in the Scriptures, but it would be a rash man indeed who could claim that it is beyond all argument that there is.

It is ironic that Catholics should feel particularly defensive concerning the knowledge-dimension of the Scriptures since they have traditionally avoided placing all their theological eggs in the scriptural basket. The Catholic emphasis upon the primacy of the community and upon its historicity lends itself to the kind of interpretation I suggest.

The great fear of those who hold out for some knowledge content in the Scriptures is, as in the other problems which I have discussed, that the *only* alternative is to see the Scriptures as a collection of subjectivistic myths resulting from the psychological projection of man's desires. I would argue that we are not confronted with the alternatives of either a hard core of knowledge, essentially untouched by psychological, historical and cultural factors, or a radical subjectivism, historicism and cultural relativism. Let me try to sketch briefly a mode of scriptural interpretation which frees it from any particular knowledge content and at the same time keeps the Scriptures from being reduced to a subjectivistic production of man. We must first of all surrender the notion of a self-contained text embodying its meaning independently of man. I would suggest viewing the Scriptures as a unique and continuing locus of the Divine-human encounter. On my hypothesis both man and the sacred text are living and thus developing. The Scriptures are a channel through which God has spoken, is speaking and will continue to speak to man. The marvel and the mystery is that though originally expressed in the language and thought patterns of a particular culture and moment in history, the Word can be heard by all men according to their development — cultural and historical, as well as personal. This means that while there

REFLECTIONS—FAITH AND METAPHYSICS 125

is continuity there is not identity of meaning and understanding. It is instead a question of a developing man and community
of which the Scriptures are also an organic and developing
factor. It should be quite evident that my hypothesis presupposes a relational and processive metaphysics. On my hypothesis
the Scriptures would not be merely the subjective projections
of man. On the other hand, they would not be books that embody meaning apart from their relation to man; they would not,
in consequence, be outside the cultural, historical and socio-
logical factors which enter into the continuing formation of
man.

The shift in perspective called for by my hypothesis affects not
only our understanding of the Scriptures, but also forces a
searching reevaluation of our traditional metaphysical language
about God. Despite the long tradition concerning the mystery
of God and his unknowability, there is also the long tradition
concerning the knowability of God, if only negatively and
analogically. I would suggest that to take seriously God as mystery involves a surrender of God as knowable, whatever the
qualifications that might be added. If we really believe that
anything said about God is immeasurably inadequate and symbolic we will constantly search for the language and symbols
that are least inadequate at this moment.

For example, we will no longer debate whether reason forces
us to affirm God as omnipotent but rather whether omnipotence
is a category that has meaning for human life. An initial response might suggest that this category is no longer meaningful because reflective men can no longer believe in a God who
is omnipotent but for reasons known only to Himself picks and
chooses when to alleviate the suffering of His children. On the
other hand, it might be possible to believe in a God who created man autonomous, who is neither a divine watchmaker nor
a divine puppeteer. The God of this faith is, then, a God of
human autonomy. The question of His omnipotence, on these
conditions, is simply irrelevant. It has nothing to do with life.
This latter view can be as empty and superficial as the traditional one; but if we believe that our religious language is not

intended to give us information about God but has as its purpose orientating, illuminating and energizing men, we can then argue for the release of possibilities in the second view not present in the first.

Finally, surrender of the Catholic's claim to absolute certainty will have profound effects on his relationship with his contemporaries. To begin with, he will recognize that the Christian has no set of answers or guarantee which places him in a privileged position of security apart from the agonizing struggles of other men. The contemporary believer does not incidentally exist in the contemporary world but is formed and structured by characteristic contemporary experience and acts within and out of rather than alongside this experience. Further, the contemporary believer has not moved beyond doubt, or nihilism, or even a certain kind of despair, but believes, acts and creates amidst all of these. Such a man will be led to acknowledge that the "presence" of God is no longer the presence that it was, or was imagined to be in other ages.

One cannot say what it might be for future ages, but here and now the presence of God takes the form of a simultaneous and terrifying absence of God.[12] Faith is *without* God. This statement cannot, of course, be taken literally (any more than could its reverse). Nor can it be absorbed within the framework of common sense or Aristotelian logic. But it is not therefore bereft of meaning. The *without* might be understood as without what has traditionally passed for God. It might be expressed in the paradox, the contemporary presence of God is His absence. We might add that only a man who can act *without* God can ever hope to encounter Him. The believer must be willing to work for values in the same way that he would just *as if* God did not exist.[13]

The believer, I suggest, must act *without* God. And so must the atheist. They share the same existential situation. That does

---

[12] Whatever the problems and difficulties it raises this surely is the experiential center from which the current "God is dead" theologians are proceeding.

[13] Here, perhaps, we have a reversal by the Christian of the Kantian *as if*.

not mean, however, that the the two merge into a single undiffer-
entiated blob. They differ principally in terms of certain values
and, more important, of the underlying vision which energizes
them. Both will share the struggle to create a new world, but
the Christian will *believe* that he is doing so through and with
an Other. The Christian of today, unlike his believing forerun-
ners, will no longer expect or seek superficial aid or comfort from
the Other, not even the certain assurance of His existence.[14] It
might be suggested that a distinct advantage of such an approach would be the avoidance of the characteristically Christian mode of self-deception, i.e., the affirmation of the noblest
values as a blind for a spiritual egotism, for a selfish individual obsession with personal immortality which the contemporary world has quite properly designated as unworthy of man.
This last will jar Christians, but if we were to put it simply we
might ask which is the more noble, a man who loves his fellowman in order to avoid hellfire or one who loves him because
he is his fellowman. This is by no means a radically new insight,
for it is already contained in the story of the saint who encountered an angel walking down the road with a torch in one
hand and a pail of water in the other. When asked what they
were for he replied, "The torch is to burn down the castles
of heaven and the water to put out the flames of hell and then
we shall see who really loves God."

---

[14] Something quite similar to what I am attempting to say has been
expressed most movingly by Michael Novak in the foreword to his recent
Belief and Unbelief (New York: The Macmillan Company, 1965). This
work came to my attention after I had completed my article and too late
for me to assimilate and integrate it adequately within my reflections. A
first perusal, however, leads me to conclude that Novak is proceeding
from experiences much like those I have described, but that he couches
them in a metaphysics different from the one I have suggested.

This Truth Sublime

JOSEPH OWENS, C. SS. R.

As Christian faith gradually sharpened its confrontation with Western metaphysics, the tendency to present God in terms of being can be seen taking progressively deeper roots. Whatever may have been the original meaning of Exodus 3:14, a current of Patristic and Scholastic thinking was stimulated by the scriptural verse to identify the nature of God with being.[1] Very strangely — from the viewpoint of the history of philosophy — this tendency developed in contrary direction to the elsewhere prevalent Neoplatonic background of Christian philosophical thought, a background that in Plotinus had expressly denied the character of being to the first principle of all things. Still more strangely — from the same viewpoint of the history of philosophy — the tendency reached a high point with St. Thomas Aquinas in the identification of the divine nature with existence. True, as far as words are concerned, St. Thomas still speaks as a rule in the vocabulary of being, not of existence. But for him being is an actuality experienced by men as contingent and incessantly changing from moment to moment, fading out into the past as it stretches on into the future.[2] St. Thomas clearly meant what in present-day vocabulary is called existence.

There was no precedent in earlier Western thought for this

---

[1] See Cornelia J. De Vogel, " 'Ego sum qui sum' et sa signification pour une philosophie chrétienne," *Revue des Sciences Religieuses*, XXV (1961), 346–354.

[2] See especially *In I Sent.*, d. 8, q. 1, a. 1, Solut. (ed. Mandonnet, I, 195) and d. 19, q. 2, a. 2, Solut. (I, 470–471).

reasoning in terms of existence. Furthermore, it ran counter to the traditional Greek understanding of being as permanence, fully as much as the identification of the omnipotent God with being had run counter to the spirit of Plotinus. Nor, as one reads St. Thomas, does one encounter attempts to tincture the "existential hyaline"[3] with anything else in order to endow it with an intelligibility not its own. Rather, existence is taken just as grasped in sensible things. It is known in judging[4] that a man or a stick or a stone exists, while in contrast a phoenix does not exist in the real world. A man has no other original knowledge of existence. No mixture of the knowledge by which he apprehends the natures of things enters into his grasp of their existence. Nothing is added to existence in its role of starting point for a long and intricate demonstration that finally reaches existence in its own nature, a nature in which the dynamic progress from past to future has vanished in the still more dynamic actuality of eternal self-possession. St. Thomas rises to lyric tones, scarcely audible through the English translation, in contemplating the God of Christian worship now brought before his intellect in terms solely of existence: "This sublime truth Moses was taught by our Lord. . . . The Lord replied 'I AM WHO AM. . . . Thou shalt say to the children of Israel: HE WHO IS hath sent me to you'" (*Contra Gentiles*, I, 22, 10; tr. Pegis). Found scattered through the theological texts of St. Thomas, this penetrating metaphysical doctrine has in our own day seen its philosophical primacy stressed by thinkers like Gilson and Fabro. It has been given, in an initial way at least, genuine philosophical presentation. It still awaits decades of painstaking metaphysical development.

---

[3] ". . . the direct interest in fattening Existence at the expense of essence. Some such loading is perhaps necessary for contemplating the existential hyaline at all, somewhat as a microscopist must stain the transparent tissues to make them visible, . . ." Donald C. Williams, "Dispensing with Existence," *The Journal of Philosophy*, LIX (1962), 754.

[4] There seems to be no satisfactory word to express this immediate grasp of existence. "Perception of existence," "intuition of existence," "apprehension of existence," "knowledge of existence," and the like, may be used. "The second operation of the intellect" and "judgment" are the standard Thomistic designations for it.

Against so inspiring and profound a background of traditional Christian thought, what is to be made of current assertions that the existence of God is unimportant, that it can be neither proven nor disproven, that to assert the existence of God is just as atheistic as to deny it,[5] that to attribute existence to God is absurd or possibly ungrammatical,[6] or that the Christian today should not seek the certain assurance of God's existence?[7] Surely, if the nature of God is existence, to deny existence to him is to deny any nature to him. It is not only the "death of God," but the stultification of the very notion. It is the reduction of the name "God" to the category of contradictions like a square circle.

To ask whether God exists, on the other hand, is undoubtedly a correctly framed question in the tradition of Christian theology. As a question, it is attested by innumerable theological treatises through the centuries. But can it also be a proper question for a metaphysician to ask? For some thinkers today, to identify God with what is concluded by a metaphysical demonstration seems little short of blasphemous. Certainly that distrust of human reason for proving God's existence clashes sharply with the attitude found in Augustine, Anselm, Bonaventure, and Aquinas. It is quite true that the great majority of present-day writers seem to accept without much question Kant's disposal of the traditional arguments for God's existence. Yet one has but to compare the text of Kant with the text of St. Thomas to see that there is not even verbal resemblance between the latter and the arguments refuted by the German philosopher. In St. Thomas the demonstration starts with sensible things existent in a real external world, and finds that these things are caused efficiently, are made to exist, by something that

---

[5] "Thus the question of the existence of God can be neither asked nor answered. If asked, it is a question about that which by its very nature is above existence, and therefore the answer — whether negative or affirmative — implicitly denies the nature of God. It is as atheistic to affirm the existence of God as it is to deny it." Paul Tillich, *Systematic Theology* (Chicago, 1951), I, 237.

[6] "And modern views make it self-evidently absurd (if they don't make it ungrammatical) to speak of such a Being and attribute existence to Him." J. N. Findlay, "Can God's Existence Be Disproved?" *Mind,* LVII (1948), 182.

[7] Eugene Fontinell, *supra,* p. 133.

is existence itself. The demonstration reaches subsistent existence first, and then finds this existence identified with the God of Christian belief.[8]

In this metaphysical procedure, accordingly, the question becomes worded in reverse order, when compared with the theological context. Having reached existence that is itself a thing and not the existence of something else, the metaphysician has still to ask "Is this subsistent existence God?" And yet, need that prevent a Christian metaphysician from legitimately posing for himself the question with the wording "Does God exist?" As a believer, he has already accepted on religious faith, with his earliest instruction, the truth that God exists. But as his intellectual scrutiny expands, is he not prompted by the desire to live this truth intellectually to the full extent of his science? If with St. Thomas he takes the path of existence in developing the science, he is led to see that the nature of being is found in subsistent existence. He does not have to be a theologian to conclude that the perfections of subsistent existence identify it beyond doubt with the God he has accepted as a believer. Has he not thereby answered his question "Can I demonstrate by reason that the God in whom I believe exists?"

The opening words of the sacred Scriptures read: "In the beginning God created the heavens and the earth" (Gen 1:1; Conf. ed.). Likewise, the first statement of the Nicene Creed is: "I believe in one God, the Father almighty, maker of heaven and earth." Similarly in the traditional catechisms the first introduction to formal Christian doctrine comes in the words "Who made the world?" or "Who made us?" with the answer "God made us," and with God presented as "the Supreme Being, infinitely perfect, who made all things and keeps them in existence" (New Baltimore Catechism). Aside from all theology, in point

---

[8] See *De Ente et Essentia*, c. IV, and the frequent occurrences of the argument in *In I Sent*. The identity of this proof with the "five ways" of the *Summa Theologiae*, I, 2, 3c, has been a subject of sharp and varied controversy. For a recent discussion, see M. Guérard des Lauriers, O.P., *La Preuve de Dieu et les Cinq Voies* (Rome, 1966), with the stages of the proof itself outlined on p. 37. Cf.: "Le rapport entre *la preuve* et *les cinq voices* est donc, simultanément, oeuvre de Dieu créant la nature raison, et oeuvre de l'homme exerçant sa propre raison." *Ibid.*, p. 6.

of fact the initiation into Christian faith through the Bible, through the creed, through traditional catechetical instruction, has been in terms of the maker of the world. The procedure takes for granted that the world in front of people is evident and admitted. The world had to be made, the reasoning follows, and its maker is called God. In this way God has been for centuries presented initially to the Christian mind. In the creed the notion of omnipotence is stressed by the insertion of the word "almighty."

Is not this a process easy enough for the as yet undeveloped mind to follow? The child knows that his building-block castles have himself as their builder. He sees oatmeal being made in the morning, dinners being cooked, houses being constructed, machines being assembled. Without his own activity his castles would not have come about, without the activity of others the things around him would not have been made. The notion that everything in front of him requires a maker, a maker who can do everything or is almighty, is not difficult for him to grasp. The whole visible world in all its broad expanse accordingly does not appear as an exception to his notion that a visible thing requires a maker. On the authority of parents and instructors he has no hesitation in accepting the identity of its maker under the name of God.

Nothing more is required for awakening the virtue of Christian faith. Reasonably, the child believes those who teach him. A sufficient and satisfactory condition is present for allowing the grace of faith to become operative and to give its firm certitude to the child's belief. As mind develops and scrutinizing questions arise, however, further intellectual equipment becomes imperative. Without regret the child drops his belief in a white-bearded Santa that puts the presents under the tree, his belief in the fairies that put a quarter under his pillow after a tooth has been extracted, his belief in the omniscience of parents and teachers, and even, after having grown up and become sufficiently mature, his belief in the essential superiority of his own race. He is faced with the question "Is my belief in the existence of God to follow the same pattern?" It turns out to be of much tougher fiber, and it faces tremendously complicated issues. As he reads Hume the status of the causal proposition, upon which his understanding of God's existence rested, comes to require deeper scrutiny. He is brought to see that he does not perceive any causing or being caused in things external to himself. Nor is he in possession of any immediately known and universal principle that would establish the need of a cause for every observed thing. As he reads Kant, the imposing of forms of his own thought upon a sensible manifold, with all its consequences of paralogism, antinomy, and incapacity to apply principles outside the world of sensible experience, offers a global challenge to his acceptance of God as the maker of the world. The still later restrictions by which logical empiricism confines human thought to the sensible world, by which phenomenology remains within the eidetic and finite, by which existentialism grounds philosophy on human intentions, or by which linguistic analysis models human reasoning upon the structure of verbal expression, all have to be faced and overcome.

Does not his faith now require an intellectual framework capable of dealing with all these? Is it not vitally in need of understanding? Has not the *fides quaerens intellectum* become a real and lived experience? Does not the initial formula "God made the world" require penetration and clarification on a metaphysical level? Does it not have to be understood now in a way that can move with ease in the intellectual circles activated by Hume and Kant and Husserl and Heidegger and Tillich and Kaufmann? Does not the more profound intellectual equipment become mandatory as an integral part of the educated Christian's life? In this intensely modern and highly developed cultural milieu is the problem posed by the opening words of Genesis, of the creed, and of the catechism to be met. Against this background does the demonstration of God's existence have to be worked out.

Where is the required mental formation and depth to be sought? Where is the training and the ability to breathe easily on the high level of contemporary thought to be obtained? Face to face with the full impact of modern thought, Leo XIII and

his successors down to the present pontiff[9] have inculcated the
necessity of mastering the thought of St. Thomas Aquinas. It is
one thing, however, to divine the direction or to catch a faint
glimmer of "the light at the other end of the tunnel." It is quite
another and much more difficult thing to follow the path step by
step. Need one wonder at the impatience with the comparatively
meager results of the efforts to reach St. Thomas' thought, at the
end of nearly a century of intense work and devoted endeavor?
Yet should one be surprised? Not only the gigantic work of establishing a critical text, as yet but half accomplished, and the
editing of enough thirteenth-century writers to supply an adequate background for assessing its thought, but also the intricate and hazardous task of reading the Thomistic principles
in their theological setting and then developing them on a strictly
metaphysical plane in accord with contemporary exigencies, will
require labor for many years to come. It is a long and difficult
work, a work to be faced seriously and carried on perseveringly.

But is the task really worth the effort? Does it actually offer
sufficient promise for satisfying the *fides quaerens intellectum?*
What advantages does it claim over other and less laborious
possibilities? At least, it provides a starting point that does not
automatically preclude its attaining the desired goal. It does
not base itself upon any finite nature, a nature that would con-
demn it irrevocably to remain within the finite order. In accord
with Aristotle, it acknowledges no other origin than sensation for
the human knowledge that comes within orbit of philosophy.
In sense experience, moreover, it sees with Aristotle that what is
directly known is an external sensible thing. The sensation itself,
as all other cognitional activity, is known only concomitantly
and reflexively. Epistemologically, there is no possibility of

9 "In this way we declare the importance of your work whose purpose
is to confront contemporary philosophy with the thinking of St. Thomas on
the problem of God. . . . the writings of St. Thomas have not ceased to
excite the interest of great minds and to promote the formation of fruitful
schools, and all the while the magisterium of the Church has been lavish
in its approbation and support of the thought of St. Thomas." Pope Paul
VI, "Address to the Thomistic Congress," Sept 10, 1965, printed in
Osservatore Romano (Sept. 13–14, 1965), tr. St. Thomas Aquinas Foundation, in *The New Scholasticism,* XL (1966), 81.

human thought becoming a starting point for reaching reality external to itself. It is already too late for that. Rather, external reality is the first object known. Known immediately and directly, it is basic for human reasoning.[10] Human cognition itself is grasped in terms of what exists externally. Far from rendering unthinkable anything that really exists outside thought, thought itself becomes thinkable only in terms of sensible things that exist outside itself. The starting point is not at all restricted to human thought and its forms.

But are not the sensible things themselves all likewise finite in nature? How can they provide a starting point that does not limit, in advance, the results of the demonstration to the finite order? The sensible things are immediately known in a two-fold way. Through conceptualization one grasps what they are, through judgment one knows that they exist. Neither of these two cognitive activities is reducible to another, even though they always accompany each other. Through conceptualization one knows objects like man, animal, tree, color, distance. All these are finite natures. They offer no possibility of reaching out to the infinite God believed in by Christian faith, the omnipotent maker of the world. The *fides quaerens intellectum* need not waste time probing them for means of understanding what it believes about God's existence. By judgment, however, one grasps the existence of these things. The typewriter, the desk, the wall, the door in front of you exist. You have but to "look out and see" in order to know that they exist. The "look out and see" is what is meant here in the technical use of the word "judgment." It is an act of knowing, an act of apprehension. What it apprehends is not part of the nature of any finite thing.[11] Existence is nowhere grasped as a nature, and accordingly is

---

[10] Strictly speaking, the thing immediately known is the end product of the stimulus and of the reaction on the part of the sensory apparatus. Distance and plurality of objects are judged as a result of habituated interpretation. But those are problems for physics and experimental psychology. The object with which the metaphysician at this stage is concerned, namely something external to human cognition and immediately known, is not affected by the further determinations and precisions.

[11] See St. Thomas, *In I Sent.*, d. 19, q. 5, a. 1, ad 7m (ed. Mandonnet, I, 489); d. 38, q. 1, a. 3, Solut. (I, 903–904). Cf. d. 8, q. 4, a. 2, Solut. (I, 222).

not a starting point that predetermines the conclusions to re-main in the finite order.

The existence grasped by judgment, moreover, is intimately conditioned by time. A cloud formation that exists at present is gone a moment later. Its fleeting existence was known through judgment at the moment, but when the formation is recon-structed by the mind it is now judged non-existent in reality. The existence of things in the sensible world is in continual change, incessant change, always going from the past through the present into the future. There is nothing static in it, not even for the smallest part of time. It is continually changing. It is radically incomplete, radically open to development, it re-quires the novelty of the future.

The existential actuality, moreover, is what is deepest and most intimate in anything.[12] None among the many specific or generic natures is indispensable for a being. The thing does not have to be a stone, or a stick, or a horse, or a man. It can be some other nature. You can do away with any particular nature in turn, and still have some other nature that is able to exist. But you cannot do away with existence, and then have anything. You can abstract from all the other aspects in turn, and still be able to have a thing. No one of them is absolutely required. But existence is required. Without existence there would not be anything. Accordingly existence is the most basic of all. Yet this most intimate actuality, the actuality on which all the other aspects are based, is in continual change. In its innermost depths any sensible thing is radically and unavoidably mutable. Small wonder St. Augustine and the long tradition following him saw mutability as the fundamental characteristic of creatures, the

---

[12] "During the whole period of a thing's existence, therefore, God must be present to it, and present in a way in keeping with the way in which the thing possesses its existence. Now existence is more intimately and profoundly interior to things than anything else. . . . So God must exist and exist intimately in everything." St. Thomas, S.T., I, 8, 1c (tr. Black-friars). Discussions of the Thomistic texts on these points may be found in my articles "The Accidental and Essential Character of Being in the Doctrine of St. Thomas Aquinas," *Mediaeval Studies*, XX (1958), 1–40; "Diversity and Community of Being in St. Thomas Aquinas," *ibid.*, XXII (1960), 257–302; and "Quiddity and Real Distinction in St. Thomas Aquinas," *ibid.*, XXVII (1965), 1–22.

characteristic that primarily distinguished creatures from God. In the very foundation of its own self, a sensible thing is change- able. It is always tending toward something new in the future. Further, insofar as existence is not part of the sensible thing's nature, what is deepest and most intimate in the thing and most required by it is accidental to it.

The combined accidentality and priority of existence to na- ture show that sensible things are dependent upon something else for their existence. Because it is accidental, in the wide sense of not belonging to their nature, the existence has to be de- pendent. Otherwise the existence would be grasped as some- thing there in itself, and not as the existence of the stone or other sensible thing. Because it is prior, it cannot be dependent on the thing it makes exist. It is accordingly dependent on some other thing. Something other, then, is making the thing exist, something that is existence itself and not the existence of some- thing else. Even though one may conjure up a series of inter- mediate causes, even a series that is circular or infinite, all the existence concerned is coming from something whose existence is neither prior nor accidental to itself, something that is identi- cal with its own existence, something that is existence itself.

This means that subsistent existence is causing by its activity the existence of all the things perceived in the external universe. Without it, they just would not be there, they would not be exist- ing. The fact that a stone or a stick is present in the world, and is known by the human mind, grounds the cogent reasoning to the conclusion that existence subsists in their ultimate cause. The consequences are apparent. Only in subsistent existence is existence to be found as a nature. As long as other things are present in the world, they are being kept in existence by the action of subsistent being. All new existence, likewise, is caused in virtue of its action. No new being comes into the world, no event happens, except by means of the action of subsistent exist- ence. Anything that exists in the external world, as well as any- thing that happens, attests the existence of subsistent being, at least to a mind that takes cognizance of the thing or event and reasons to the entailed metaphysical conclusions.

It is not too difficult to show that subsistent existence is identified with the God of Christian worship, the God introduced in
the opening verse of Genesis, professed in the first words of the
creed, and taught in the initial question of the catechism, the
God in whom "we live and move and have our being."[13] As the
ultimate source of existence for everything else, subsistent being
is clearly identical with the God who made heaven and earth.
As concurring in every action, from the standpoint of all new
existence produced, subsistent being is unmistakably the God
in whom we live and move. As the conserving cause of all existence outside itself, it is equally the God in whom we have our
being. In giving being to all things and events, subsistent existence is likewise identical with the divine providence without
which no sparrow falls to the ground. As most intimate to every
thing and every action, subsistent being is obviously one with
the searcher of hearts and with the Lord who inclines a human
heart in whatever direction he pleases. It is the cause of every
free action and decision. In all these aspects, subsistent being
shows itself to be identical with the revealed God of Scripture.

Yet all this metaphysical knowledge of subsistent being is
founded upon what is originally known through judgment. It is
not founded on anything first known through conceptualization.
Accordingly, one has no authentic concept of existence. To be
thought about and discussed, what is known through judgment
has to be conceptualized under other notions, such as something,
or actuality, or perfection. All the more, then, does one lack an
authentic concept of subsistent being, or of anything one attributes to it on its own level. What subsistent being is, what
goodness or truth or justice is when attributed to subsistent being
and thereby identified with it, we just do not know.[14]
From the viewpoint of conceptual knowledge one's ignorance of

---

[13] Acts 17:28. For St. Thomas' use of this scriptural text, see *In 1 Sent.*,
d. 36, q. 1, a. 3, ad 4m (ed. Mandonnet, I, 837), and *S.T.*, I, 18, 4, ad 1m.

[14] See St. Thomas *S.T.*, I, 13, 2, ad 2m. St. Thomas frequently (e.g.,
De Ver., II, 11c; *De Pot.*, VII, 5c; CG, IV, 7) stresses that everything
in God is God's being or substance. On the background for the Thomistic
doctrine of the divine unknowability, see A. C. Pegis, "Penitus Manet
Ignotum," *Mediaeval Studies*, XXVII (1965), 212–226.

subsistent being and everything in it is total. From this stand-point one can apply to the full the negative theology of Christian tradition, that God remains utterly unknown, entirely unknown, is as nothing, and so on. In terms of conceptual knowledge, one's ignorance is complete.

In terms of what is originally known through judgment, how-ever, one's knowledge of God can become extremely rich. The whole positive theology, as found developed at such great length in St. Thomas, follows from the demonstrated conclusion that existence subsists. Existence in its first and literal sense is thereby shown to be the nature of God. There is no possibility here of symbol or metaphor. Existence, as we know it in sensible things and in ourselves, has its nature only in God. It has its nature solely in subsistent being. Literally, *what* existence is can be found nowhere except in its primary instance. The exist-ence found in creatures, while of course existence in a literal sense, is only a secondary grade. The primary, the first literal sense of existence, is found solely in God.

This reflection holds likewise for all other perfections that are capable of actual identity with subsistent being. In their pri-mary and model sense they are literally present in it. So truth, in its literal sense, is present in God. So is goodness, and justice, and wisdom. The instances of these that we immediately ex-perience in the world around us are only secondary instances. Other attributes, attributes that involve imperfection in their very notion, are in God only causally or metaphorically, as when God is called a tower of strength or a rock of salvation. But existence and perfections like intelligence, action, providence, justice, are in God in their literal and primary meaning, a literal meaning known to us through its secondary instances.

In all the really important things, accordingly, the meta-physical principles of St. Thomas enable one to speak literally in applying perfections to God. Even though one does not know what these perfections are when identified with subsistent being, one knows nevertheless that they are present in God in their full and literal sense. The tendency to lump together the two adjec-tives in the statement "anything said about God is immeasurably inadequate and symbolic"[15] does not at all follow when faith finds understanding in the light of St. Thomas' metaphysical principles. "Immeasurably inadequate" our knowledge of God certainly is. But in the really important metaphysical characteristics it is not at all symbolic. It is literal, and indicates the primary literal sense of these characteristics.

In this way, then, the *fides quaerens intellectum* penetrates metaphysically into the content of the faith's most primitive teaching, the teaching that God made the world. The profound reasoning of St. Thomas is but an amplification on the philosophical level of the first truth learned in catechism. Mastering his principles is the intellectual process of growing up in the life that received its infant nourishment through authoritative instruction from parents and teachers. Developing them to their far-reaching conclusions is the work of intellectual maturity in the Christian seeking understanding of what he believes. The Thomistic metaphysical principles show upon scrutiny that they do not restrict conclusions to the sensible or even finite world. They accordingly offer prospect of reaching metaphysical knowledge of God. Examination of their actual performance shows that they accomplish this objective, even though they still require long years of painstaking development. Found in St. Thomas in theological contexts, they await thoroughly metaphysical organization. But even in their original setting they are clear enough in their philosophical message, when they are patiently collected and compared and studied. From the existence known directly through judgment in sensible things they proceed with sure step to the sublime truth that in God existence and nature are identical.

Will not this truth sublime, with its manifold implications, have real bearing upon a Christian's spiritual life? The realization that existence is the nature of God both shocks routine complacency and stimulates appreciation of one's own shared

---

[15] Eugene Fontinell, *supra*, p. 132. For a discussion of the Thomistic way of predicating concepts of God, in contrast to the symbolic, see Lewis S. Ford, "Tillich and Thomas: The Analogy of Being," *The Journal of Religion*, XLVI (1966), 229–245.

existence. Explaining St. Bernard's dictum "God is the being, not essential but causal, of all things," St. Thomas concludes: ". . . . therefore divine being, from which all created being flows by way of efficiency and exemplification, is called the being of all things."[16] In saying that existence flows from God, one may have difficulty in avoiding the notion of formally determined sequence, as water flows from a spring, conclusions from premises, consequences from grounds, or instantiation from a basic notion. In logic one becomes accustomed to think in terms of formal sequence of one truth from another, and may tend unwittingly to reduce existential sequence to the same type. Or in thinking of existence as participated, one may unconsciously represent it as a form shared by all existents, quite as the color red is shared by all things red. A distinct effort is required to show one's self that one shares existence not by the addition of any new quality or form, but entirely by being made to be. When subsistent existence makes anything exist, it adds nothing by way of nature. It just makes the thing itself exist, by way of efficient causality. This is altogether different from the addition of a new form, as in the case of grace. Yet the existence that all creatures possess has its nature only in God. The very existence regularly taken for granted, squandered at times, often unappreciated, continually changing, continually passing, is the very being of God — not formally, but in the sequence of efficient causality. Existence, however, is what is most intimate to one's self. It is the very core of all else. As giving it continually, God is understood to be working most intimately within us, interiorly to all we are, at the very center around which all else in us evolves. Existence is most intimate in our make-up, and God is its interior cause. Can the notion of the presence of God be brought any closer or made any more manifest? Where existence is exercised, there is God.

Likewise, is not the realization that one's existence continuously depends upon the exercise of God's conserving causality

---

[16] *In 1 Sent.*, d. 8, q. 1, a. 2, Solut. (ed. Mandonnet, I, 198). On the topic, see G. B. Phelan, "The Being of Creatures," *Proceedings of the American Catholic Philosophical Association,* XXXI (1957), 118–125.

geared to driving home the Christian notions of one's continued
and total need for the divine power? Does it not strongly support
and make intelligible the specifically Christian teachings about
the virtue of humility? Since all new existence comes from God,
and is imparted in virtue of the divine activity, one cannot raise
a finger, draw a breath, speak a word, except in the causality of
the God in whom one lives and moves and has one's being. The
very fact that one raises an eyebrow means under metaphysical
scrutiny that God is here and now exercising His activity as primary movent, and is doing so as the intimately present subsistent
existence from which all new existence flows. How can the
realization of all this help but make one walk more closely with
God? Where new existence is being imparted, there is God
working as its efficient cause, interiorly and intimately.

These considerations enter even more forcibly into the understanding of one's own free activity. A nature that is existence is
not confined by any formally determining limits. Operating in
an order superior to and transcending the alternatives of necessity and contingence,[17] it moves the free will of man infallibly
to the smallest detail of every decision and action without in any
way forcing or determining. Every finite cause, on the other
hand, determines the caused activity's course as it moves something else to action. But subsistent existence is not a finite
nature. In causing the activity appropriate to a free agent, it
does not determine the activity. Rather, it gives the exercise of
the creature's freedom. A free action would be unintelligible if
its actuality, as free, had its ultimate explanation in a finite
nature like man or angel. It could be merely accepted as a
psychological fact, and left without philosophical explanation.
But as understood through primary origin in the motion by an
infinite nature, subsistent being, its entire freedom is philo-

---

[17] See St. Thomas, *In I Perherm.*, lect. 14, Leonine no. 22. To say that
existence as a nature operates or performs activities, need not run counter to
good grammar. An abstract form of a word stands without difficulty as the
subject of a transitive verb; e.g., "Kindness wins friends." As existence in
creatures is never a nature, it cannot in them be the subject of any
operation or activity. But where it is subsistent as a nature, there is no
reason why it should not be the subject of the sentence even when the
verb is transitive.

sophically guaranteed. True, one cannot know *what* God's moving of the free will is, any more than one knows what anything else in God is. One cannot conceptualize it. But one knows that it is there, and that to act in this way pertains to the nature of subsistent being. The sublimity, the responsibility, of a free decision and free activity are thrust home with pertinent force under these considerations.

Illumined by this metaphysically known truth, how can the omnipotence of God fail to be of importance for one's daily life? The thought that every wave of a finger, every breath, is so intimately dependent on God's omnipotence, working interiorly at the core of one's self and one's activity, keenly sharpens one's appreciation of routine activity. The realization that every act of free will is taking place only in virtue of the divine omnipotence, makes one duly sensitive to the presence of God and his providence. Does not this enable one to understand the traditional Christian prayer of petition? Even the smallest thing, like a sparrow falling to the ground, comes under the all-embracing scope of divine providence and omnipotence. To pray for the quick finding of a misplaced note, for relief from an ailment, for courage to face a difficult situation, becomes readily intelligible. Nor is there anything odd, when one views things in the light of the divine omnipotence, in believing that the course of natural events has been from all eternity adapted to fit the object one prays for, and that the course of nature would have been different if one had not so prayed? To the divine omnipotence the task of arranging the sequence of events in accord with the objects prayed for is no more difficult than to have arranged it in some other way. What is particularly surprising about that? The understanding of all other existence as caused by subsistent existence makes the Christian tradition on the necessity of abundant prayer of petition readily acceptable.

Against this metaphysical background, can the *fides quaerens intellectum* hesitate at all in giving an affirmative answer to the question (Fontinell, *supra*, p. 132) "whether omnipotence is a category that has meaning for human life"? Does not faith thereby reach understanding of its teaching about the total de-

144 SPEAKING OF GOD

pendence of creatures on God? Its insistence on the need of frequent prayer will be more deeply inculcated and more intel-
ligently embraced. The power of the Pantokrator,[18] as handed
down in Christian tradition, is shown to be fully adequate to
the task of answering prayer. Why should not that power be
continually exercised even in the smallest details?

Similarly the metaphysical grasp of existence, in accord with
the principles of St. Thomas, safeguards intellectually the traditional Christian motivation of eternal reward and avoidance
of eternal punishment. It provides the understanding of the
Christian virtue of hope. Existence, grasped through judgment,
is conceptualized as a perfection upon which transcendental
properties follow. These are attributes like truth and goodness
and beauty. To have any of them, you must first have a thing,
a thing that exists. Upon the thing's existence the transcendental
properties are based. In this way truth and beauty and goodness
are understood not as detached "values," but as real properties
of real things. To have them, one must first have the things.
Without the things, the properties just cannot be had. The desire for the things, then, becomes the rational way of striving
for the enjoyment of the properties. The possession of the
things is the reward. Accordingly, the *fides quaerens intellectum*
is able to understand and retain the traditionally instilled
Christian motivation. One lives and works for the reward of
heaven, one strives to avoid the eternal punishment and horror
of hell. Such is the way God wishes to be served, according
to the practice of Christian faith. He wishes man to be united
with him in the beatific vision of heaven, and not separated
from him in an abyss of everlasting frustration. Knowing through
faith that God has so planned things, one is able to give full intellectual acceptance to the reward-punishment type of motivation, even when acting through the supernatural virtue of charity
for the supreme overall purpose of pleasing God.

Nor is one's appreciation of human life in any way dim-
inished by regarding men as objects that share existence through

---

[18] On this notion of the Pantokrator as expressing the "common heritage,"
see John Courtney Murray, *The Problem of God* (New Haven and London,
1964), pp. 34–35.

the causality of God. One reasons to the spiritual nature of man from his intellectual activities. Man thinks on the plane of the universal and with complete reflection. The grasp of the universal calls for scientific knowledge and for freedom of will and of action. It signalizes man as a free agent, whose every authentically human action is a fresh and independent start, a novelty. Brought directly into actuality by the divine omnipotence, without possibility of intermediate cause, the new beginning in the order of events, as introduced by a human act, attests both the superiority of men over non-intellectual agents, and the essential immediacy of man's relation to God. Meant to know God through intellect and to serve him freely through will, every individual man is raised above the conditions that allow merely material things to be possessed as property. Over human life and its propagation man does not have proprietary dominion. In questions of homicide, including suicide, war, legal execution, mercy killing, duelling, abortion, and hunger strikes, in questions of mutilation and slavery, in questions of marriage and education, the divine will as known through the authority that speaks for it on earth has to be respected in every detail. The philosophical principles of St. Thomas are of crucial significance here for *understanding* the attitude of the Church in regard to all these questions, even when her stand runs counter to almost universally accepted social opinion, such as with duelling in the eighteenth century or with today's controversial issues on human life and its propagation.

The need for these Thomistic metaphysical principles is just as urgent for bringing about a wholehearted acceptance, by the faith, of today's scientifically established views on the nature of the sensible universe. In these Thomistic principles does not the evolutionary concept of nature and of man find a most appropriate metaphysical setting? Existence, as grasped through judgment, is continually changing in man and in sensible things. It is always progressing. It does not stay still for a moment. The deepest core of visible things is consequently in unceasing flux, and it is being given continually from within. When scientists, in explaining on their own level the evolution of nature, say they

brook no interference from without, one can fully agree. But
the action of subsistent existence is emphatically from within.
Far from interference, it is what is most essentially required
by the natures of things. One may therefore expect God to give
existence as the natures of things demand. If they require evolution, existence will be given them in exactly that way. When the
proper moment comes for animation by a spiritual soul, the
soul will be created without any interference from outside,
without any discontinuity for the viewpoint of orderly progress.
God continues to dispense existence as the natures of things
require. For his omnipotence there is no more interference in
creating a human soul at the moment the natural evolution of
the body demands it, than in imparting new existence in the
rustling of a leaf as brought about by atmospheric conditions.
Nor, from the viewpoint of his omnipotence, is there anything
stranger in the one exercise of his activity than in the other.

The *fides quaerens intellectum,* then, urgently requires a deep
appreciation and a correct understanding of the divine omnipotence, as it faces today's intellectual problems about both
man and nature. It has in this regard a strong need that can be
satisfied by the metaphysical explanation of omnipotence in
terms of subsistent being, the existence that gives being to all
else. In the principles of St. Thomas it finds this explanation.
Gauged from their viewpoint, can divine omnipotence fail to
be a most meaningful category for human life, both in daily
activities and in the intellectual confrontation with the chal-
lenges of the modern world?

The above reflections underscore the necessity of more widespread and deeper understanding of the Thomistic metaphysical
principles for the faith, as it is lived in today's culture. Against
that background, what is to be made of the recent suggestion
(Fontinell, *supra,* p. 107) that in continuing to think in terms
of "traditional realistic metaphysics," the Church cannot assimilate "the new discoveries of philosophy and science," and "may
be heading for a metaphysical Galileo case"? In the historic
Galileo case, the clash occurred between the legitimate pro-
gram of experimental science and the unjustifiable adhesion

to the traditional Aristotelian contention that scientific knowledge of natural activities and properties could be obtained
from knowledge of their substantial forms. Aristotle had outlined the contention in unmistakable terms in the long opening
chapter of the *Parts of Animals*. The teaching of St. Thomas,
running through all the periods of his writing, is on the contrary that the specific differences of natural things are impervious to human knowledge.[19] If that teaching had been followed through and appreciated in the sixteenth century, there
would have been no clash with experimental science. Rather,
philosophy would have cleared the way for the progress of the
new and fast developing sciences, and would have shown them
how to keep themselves integrated in the overall complex of
human knowledge.

If Fontinell's parallel means anything, then, it indicates that
the best way of avoiding a "metaphysical Galileo case" is deeper
understanding of and more widespread adhesion to the metaphysical principles of St. Thomas. Drawing out and applying
their consequences will mean showing a Christian how to understand what he believes, amidst present scientific and philosophical developments. In regard to St. Thomas, if included
under "traditional realistic metaphysics," the conclusion should
be just the opposite of that which Fontinell himself would apparently like to draw.

On the other hand, the understanding of God, in terms of the
existence immediately known through judgment, safeguards
the legitimate and keenly felt opposition to any genuinely conceptual knowledge of God. There is little need for fear that
copious metaphysical reasoning about God will do away with
mystery in the divine existence, or for thinking that "to take
seriously God as mystery involves a surrender of God as knowable" (Fontinell, *supra*, p. 132), or that "since the late Middle

[19] For a list of passages, see M.-D. Roland-Gosselin, *Le "De Ente et
Essentia de S. Thomas d'Aquin*, reprint (Paris, 1948), p. 40, n. 2. For
discussions, see R. B. Gehring, "The Knowledge of Material Essences
according to St. Thomas Aquinas," *The Modern Schoolman*, XXXIII
(1956), 153–181; J. Owens, "St. Thomas Aquinas and Modern Science,"
Transactions of the Royal Society of Canada, Fourth Series, I (1963),
283–293.

Ages there has been a greater and greater tendency to freeze the unlimited mystery and possibilities of the faith within a particular metaphysic" (*supra*, p. 127). No "particular metaphysic" dominated even the Scholastic tradition, a tradition that from a philosophical standpoint was radically pluralistic. The ever present controversies testify eloquently enough to this. Nor did any recognized Scholastic metaphysics tend to limit the possibilities of mystery. The distinction between faith and reason, grace and nature, was zealously upheld. Nor, from the viewpoint that is of interest in the present discussion, can the various Scholastic metaphysics be grouped together in contrast to the modern ones. In the tenet that being is other than that which is, St. Thomas falls in more with Heidegger than with Aristotle, and in maintaining that what is most basic in sensible things is always flowing he is more in accord with Bergson than with Scotus. In regard to the ontological argument he is classed with Kant rather than with Anselm.

The profound role of mystery, in fact, has never been sidestepped in genuine Scholastic tradition. The providence that permits so much apparently undeserved suffering and so much evil in the world remains inscrutable. In the metaphysics of St. Thomas, providence is shown to be always at work in the events of the world. Yet what providence is on the divine level remains, like every other perfection in God, utterly unknown to men. The supernatural aspects of God, such as the Trinity, and what is participated through grace, remain entirely above metaphysical penetration. In no way can subsistent existence be grasped metaphysically under the aspect of a nature. There is not the faintest danger that metaphysical reasoning will remove mystery in regard to knowledge of God.

Nor is there any room for objecting that a static cast will arise in the form of "eternal and immutable essences" (Fontinell, *supra, p.* 113). Common essences or natures, as one reading of St. Thomas' *De Ente et Essentia* should suffice to show, are but abstractions. Only individuals exist in the real world. What is abstracted as a universal exists nowhere but in the human mind. But the essence or nature as such does not exist at all.

Specifically, the natural essences are impenetrable to the human mind. Much more so is the changeable singular thing, the only thing that exists in sensible reality. There is not the least reason, accordingly, for fearing any opposition to organic evolution and cosmic development in St. Thomas' teaching on essence. The specific natures of sensible things cannot be known by way of substantial form. They can be known only as manifested by their activities, and these are explained by the experimental sciences. Since for St. Thomas existence is basic and in sensible things is ever changing with time, "change which goes to the very root of being" (Fontinell, *supra*, p. 112) dominates the sensible universe. From change, however, is excluded the nature of being, subsistent existence. There are no new real relations in God. Yet every giving of being is new, from the standpoint of what comes into existence, and every free decision is a new start in the order of events, a new beginning that nothing going before it was able to determine.

Substance, of course, remains untouched. The original Aristotelian term for it was *ousia*, being*ness*. As long as you have any being at all, you have substance in the Scholastic sense. Where a man remains the same person from infancy to old age, while changing in size, weight, color, and habits, the distinction between himself and these accidental characteristics will remain. But to suggest on this ground that Thomistic metaphysics is "fundamentally realistic and substantialistic" (Fontinell, *supra*, p. 108) runs counter to all that has just been considered about the role of existence in St. Thomas. Existence is clearly what is basic. More fundamental than the real thing, it actuates both the real and the cognitional, and is necessarily presupposed by either order. Epistemologically, it is grasped as an accident, for in sensible things it has accidental status. What is most fundamental in sensible things is for Thomistic metaphysics not a substance, but an accidental perfection.

So far, it should be quite evident, philosophy has played little part in the *aggiornamento*. As has been remarked (*America*, June 12, 1965), "a dozen other aspects . . . have gotten all the headlines — liturgy, the vernacular, canon law, ecumenism, . . ."

(p. 841). It is still hard to see signs that philosophy will play a greater part in the near future. It is just possible, however, as the editorial note in *America* suggested, that the philosophical issue may be the "sleeper" here, and "the most far-reaching, potentially explosive debate of all." Should that come to be the actual situation in the near future, the need of bringing the Thomistic metaphysical principles to a stage of development in which they will be able to cope with the situation is clear. The possibility of a "metaphysical Galileo case" calls for renewed efforts at deeper penetration into the thought of St. Thomas, and its wider spread in the Catholic intellectual circles of today.

Realizing to the full, then, that "worthwhile things were nevertheless being produced on the other islands" (Fontinell, *supra,* p. 100), need one be blind to the fact that worthwhile things, perhaps much more worthwhile for one's overall purposes, have been produced in one's own territory? Do not the above reflections show that in our own tradition there is content eminently worth being developed and put to the service of the *fides quaerens intellectum?* From this viewpoint does not the philosophical path indicated by the principles of St. Thomas for proving the existence of God have an extremely pertinent bearing on present-day thought? Why should not the effort and the time be devoted to organizing and developing those principles on a thoroughly metaphysical level? What better prospect is there, in particular, for faith seeking understanding of the initial truth of Bible and creed, a truth accepted in the literal sense of the words, the truth that God made the world?

Nor does the adhesion to St. Thomas' principles with full accord exclude in the least the much appreciated contributions of other philosophies. The intricate tools of modern logics, the phenomenological approaches that escape dichotomies such as subjective and objective, the studies of the various existentials like dread and ultimate concern, the close scrutinies of language, do not at all supplant or hinder the progress of Thomistic metaphysics. They are perfectly compatible with it. There is of course no question of absorption of any one of these philosophies in the others. Each stands on its own feet. Each can understand, appreciate, and learn from the others, without being overwhelmed or suffocated. Eidetic aspects can be abstracted and studied and used as starting points for profitable development of thought, with existence in the Thomistic sense disregarded. Existentials are there. They can be explored and used as a basis for thinking, with fascinating and helpful results. Language may be analyzed, and logic applied, with increased light on human thought processes.

Why should not these other ways of thinking be welcomed? To some minds, Scholastic metaphysics seems to have no appeal. There are thoughtful people who can be motivated, even to heroic sacrifice of life on the battlefield or in freedom agitations, by self-grounded values. For them Thomistic metaphysics and its use in moral philosophy may have little meaning. For others the vivid and poignant style of existentialism seems required to sustain a continued process of philosophical thought. Others prefer to remain in the abstract order of logic, or in the conceptual thinking that is easier for the mind's natural bent. What is there in the Thomistic principles to prevent all these from going each his own way? Does not Thomistic thought, rather, explain clearly what each of these is doing, and show one how to appreciate, deeply, the results of their labors? How, then, does it not guarantee freedom and support to them all? By the same token, however, it insists on corresponding freedom for itself. How can any of these thought processes hinder or affect adversely the fundamental Thomistic way of reaching God from sensible creatures, of explaining in their literal sense the opening words of Genesis, of establishing metaphysically the sublime truth that God is his existence?

Nor should Thomistic preference have the least fear that new thought forms or the developing sensible universe will in the future undermine or alter its metaphysical principles. New discoveries will always be welcome and stimulating. Yet as long as there is a stick to move a stone, as long as a flame or an element warms a pot of water, as long as a leaf rustles in the wind, and a human intellect takes cognizance of any of this, the way remains paved for reaching subsistent existence in accord with the principles of St. Thomas. Even if the universe and man evolve to a point where everything as now known has changed beyond recognition, even if all material things be sublimated into the pure subjectivity of human thought, nevertheless, as long as the human intellect notes the consummation of the process and reflects upon its own cognition of it, it has still all the necessary equipment to reason demonstratively to the existence of God.

There is no philosopichally tenable reason, therefore, why the magnificent developments of modern thought should require the exclusion of Thomistic metaphysics. Rather, this metaphysics is a way of thinking that can live in profitable harmony with them and fill needs they professedly cannot satisfy, especially in their acknowledged inability to demonstrate God's existence by means of metaphysical principles. Even though for the reasons just outlined there will always be people who will prefer to remain in pastures that the human intellect finds more natural for its thinking, such as the realm of concepts or of vivid existentials, there will likewise be people whose faith seeking understanding will have need for Thomistic metaphysics. Should not the culture of the others be broad enough to recognize the place of St. Thomas for the *fides quaerens intellectum?* Can anything justify the efforts to deny his thought the full rights of citizenship in the modern intellectual community?

True, there is no suggestion of drawing up in legislative form a "tight code" (Fontinell, *supra*, p. 99) that would ban the teaching or learning or developing of Thomistic metaphysics. Yet is it not tantamount to a prohibition to instill into readers the unproved and unprovable suggestion that as a "traditional realistic metaphysics" Thomistic thought "has had its day," that "its world of substantial things and unchanging essences and absolutely certain knowledge of them is already in the past and irrevocably so" (Fontinell, *supra*, p. 107)? Does not this insinuate that Thomistic metaphysics is somehow outmoded? Is it not a stigma sufficient to turn immature and uninformed minds away from the study of St. Thomas? Does it not imply, for a student about to enter philosophy or a seminarian preparing for theology, that dedication to Scholastic philosophy means second-class citizenship in the contemporary intellectual world?

What is the real situation? If by "traditional realistic metaphysics" is meant Scholastic metaphysics or Thomistic metaphysics, the above suggestions are palpably wrong. Is it too much to say that there is not, as yet, and never has been in the past, an authentic Scholastic metaphysics?[20] In the sense of a philosophy organized in its own right, Scholastic metaphysics is still very much a thing of the future. It is emphatically not something of the past. It is something to be worked for, something to be developed. In particular the metaphysical principles of St. Thomas, introduced as occasion demanded throughout his theological writings, lie open to wondrous prospects of development. Far from an accomplishment of the past, their philosophical organization and expansion still lie in the future. This is a challenge. It is a challenge that is actually being accepted. In the same sense in which Plato and Aristotle are "never so alive as today,"[21] the thinking out, on the philosophical level, of the principles of St. Thomas continues to be something vital and contemporary.

Is it not surprising, then, to be told today that the untiring labors of men like Grabmann and Ehrle have no relevance for the contemporary renewal, that the editing of a few more medieval Quodlibeta is unimportant for the present needs? Men so concerned with relevance do not seem to see the relevance of critical editions of St. Thomas now being undertaken with renewed vigor at Yale and other centers, and of the publication of lesser medieval documents that are necessary to provide the background against which the Thomistic and other leading Scholastic texts are to be understood. The availability of these is imperative if the philosophical principles of St. Thomas are to be correctly developed in our own day and in the future.

Nor need there be any dread of second-class citizenship if one's formation and adhesions are Scholastic. In the genial atmosphere

---

[20] See Anton Pegis, *The Middle Ages and Philosophy* (Chicago, 1963), and *"Sub Ratione Dei:* A Reply to Professor Anderson," *The New Scholasticism,* XXXIX (1965), 141–157.

[21] John Herman Randall, Jr., *Aristotle* (New York, 1960), p. viii.

that pervades present-day American philosophical circles, no one is excluded if he has something worth saying. In this respect the mastery of Scholastic philosophy is a welcome entry card. Particularly for university staffs are experts on medieval philosophy in demand.

It has been objected that seminarians and students cannot learn both Scholastic philosophies and modern philosophies in their two or three short years of study. Of course they cannot master even one philosophy in that short time, be the philosophy an existentialism, a phenomenology, or linguistic analysis. They can, however, become acquainted with all the major ways of thinking, and in the order and relative emphasis that will best serve their later needs. Fundamental from this viewpoint is their acquaintance with the depth in which the principles of St. Thomas minister to the *fides quaerens intellectum*. The most a seminarian can be given in two or three short years is a map of the way, with the prospect of acquainting himself more and more with the field as he pursues his theological studies and ripens his thought in the reading of later years. He should be well enough acquainted to have deep respect for the worth and cogency of the Thomistic demonstrations, no matter how faintly he sees "the light at the other end of the tunnel." At least he will not leave with the superficial notion that he has seen through flaws in the demonstration of God's existence.

Acquaintance with other ways of thinking may well serve other needs. All sorts of mentalities are required to make a world. Some seminarians and Catholic students are just not attracted by Scholastic ways of thinking. If phenomenological description and concern with existentials is more profitable for these, the newer ways of thought lie open. But that is no reason why respect for Scholasticism and a general appreciation of what it has to offer should not be part of their education. In this regard they can be made to see — and without too much difficulty — that reasoning based upon eidetic aspects can never result in a demonstration of the existence of God, for by the very finite and formal character of its starting points it is excluded from reaching the uncreated. Similarly reasoning on the basis of existentials may be inspiring and profitable, but by the restriction of its starting point to subjectivity it is rendered unable to develop a metaphysical demonstration of God's existence. For the faith seeking understanding of its belief that God in the literal sense made the world, the way is that marked out by St. Thomas. Genuine freedom to be presented and learned and appreciated and developed is all that Thomistic metaphysics asks, but it can accept nothing less.

These views, one may further object, judge all knowledge by the principles of St. Thomas. That is true. But no one can philosophize in a vacuum. You have to take your start from some principles. But the principles should be broad enough and deep enough to allow recognition of the legitimacy of other principles as primary starting points, even though personally one cannot accept them in that role. One can nevertheless acknowledge them as truths, with their own inherent intelligibility. In point of fact, things exist in reality, are conceived in thought, and are expressed in language. Principles found in things, principles found in thought, and principles found in language have accordingly been used by the many different philosophies as their respective starting points. In the way in which these different principles are given the basic position in the different philosophies, they will mark the subsequent course of the thought with a characteristic direction and spirit. They will give rise to radically different philosophies. But in each case the principles should be open enough to allow a clear-sighted vision of other starting points for other intellectual worlds. At the same time they should keep one keenly and uncompromisingly aware of the all-pervading differences between one's own philosophy and other philosophies. The hundred eyes of Argus are constantly required to enable a philosophy to see in all directions at once and to be alert in maintaining a balanced outlook in a pluralistic universe.

The metaphysical principles of St. Thomas eminently satisfy this last criterion. As the noosphere, to use Teilhard de Chardin's apt coinage, spreads with increased opportunities for education, the necessity of providing for the *fides quaerens intellectum* in cultured Christians becomes greater. Not the least is the requirement of knowledge about God. Particularly in this respect are the broad and ever open principles of St. Thomas the answer to the challenge in the recent versions of the Zarathustrian tidings that God is dead.

What, then, is God, literally, in terms open to human understanding? God is existence, and existence, where it subsists, is God. That is the *sublima veritas* reached in the conclusion of the Thomistic demonstration that God is his existence. The collocation of the words in the Latin gives "sublime" the emphatic place in the expression. This would be matched in English by correspondingly reversing the usual collocation and translating *haec sublima veritas* by "this truth sublime." It is a truth that brings intellectual maturity to the *fides quaerens intellectum*. Faith no more depends upon one's understanding in maturity than in childhood, but it does seek the understanding appropriate to each successive stage of life. The Catholic intellectual does wish to understand what he believes, as far as human reason can go. In tenets open to intellectual scrutiny he does wish to be intellectually secure. In St. Thomas are to be found the satisfactory principles for this task. Confronted with the broad and ever developing expanse of modern thought, should the educated Catholic, seeking to understand his faith, be cut off from this invaluable assistance? Should the *fides quaerens intellectum*, endeavoring to probe in the crucial contemporary circumstances the literal meaning of God as maker of the world, as presented in the opening words of Genesis and of the creed, be deprived of the intellectual penetration afforded by the truth sublime that what God is is his existence?

Postscript by Eugene Fontinell to Father Owens' Article

Father Owens' article, from my perspective, is a good example of the kind of realistic metaphysics that, despite Father Owens' distinctions and refinements, is not only in sharp contrast but also in opposition to the dominant strand of contemporary thought and experience. It would not be appropriate for me, nor possible within the confines of a brief postscript, to respond to every point of difference between Father Owens' position and mine. I do think, however, that a few comments might help to focus a little better the issues involved.

First, I do not claim to be able to "prove" that "traditional realistic metaphysics . . . has had its day." I firmly believe that it has but I admit the possibility that "this may in fact be a contemporary delusion" (p. 107). If I read Father Owens correctly he is not even willing to admit the *possibility* of the demise of the metaphysics to which he adheres. I concede that since for him "Scholastic metaphysics is still very much a thing of the future" it would be difficult for him to admit its demise.

Second, though I affirm both the possibility and probability that "traditional metaphysics has had its day," I immediately add that "it will always be necessary to account for certain of its basic insights" (p. 107). Nothing I have said can be properly read as saying or even implying "that the untiring labors of men like Grabmann and Ehrle have no relevance for the contemporary renewal" (p. 162 of Owens' essay). It would be an even graver misreading of my article to conclude that I am patronizing a thinker of the stature of Aquinas or that I hold that we can dispense with the study of medieval thought. I readily concede the relevance of Aquinas to contemporary life, as I concede the relevance of Plato or Descartes. The issue, however, is whether the true relevance of the great thinkers of the past is to be discovered by encountering them in the fullness of their historical and cultural context (with its accompanying limitations), or by sifting out certain aspects of their thought which assertedly are known with absolute certainty as principles capable of perennial development.

Third, Father Owens says that "Genuine freedom to be presented and learned and appreciated and developed is all that Thomistic metaphysics asks." I heartily agree that such freedom should be accorded Thomistic metaphysics. I do not agree, however, that within the Roman Catholic community this freedom has been denied. I have serious doubts that the freedom which Father Owens asks for Thomistic metaphysics is also extended to other philosophies by the leaders of Roman Catholi-

cism. It is not sufficient to grant that non-Thomistic philosophers
are not all bad or even that they have grasped truths not achieved
by Thomism. The biting issue is whether a Roman Catholic
thinker is free to pursue his philosophy even when that brings
him into fundamental conflict with Thomistic philosophy and the
theology which has developed from that philosophy.

Finally, I never said nor meant to imply that the existence of
God is unimportant. The question is whether the existence of
God — or better, the reality of God — is inseparable from man's
ability to prove it. The possibility of proving God's existence is
a philosophical problem and weighty thinkers are ranged on both
sides of the question. My assertion is that this philosophical
problem cannot be settled by the Church but that this does not,
or at least should not, jeopardize our *faith* in God.